F*#KING MARKETING

The true story of an international arms dealer, whose insane
marketing capabilities landed him in Federal Prison, and how
your business revenue can exponentially grow because of it!

GUARANTEED!!

BY
Ethan Erhardt

Original cover image: wallpapercave.com

Intro

I'm an Israeli-American international arms dealer, and Federal Prison sucks! But this is not the end of the story. It's true. Every damn bit of it. However, so I don't end up permanently disappearing, I was advised by my attorney to forgo some specific details regarding my case. Well, some of them. And this is not even close to the end. It just seemed like a really great place to start before I go back to the beginning of the story. How did I wind up where I'm at (the Federal Prison part)? Exceptionally great marketing. I've had no formal training and have been incredibly successful at everything I've ever done. You tell me something can't be done, and I'll show you five ways it can be. I'm that damn good.

Chapter 1

I came from a place where nothing itself was so expensive, that we couldn't even afford that. We actually had less than nothing. If that's somehow even possible. Not only did we have nothing, but I knew even less than what we had. For example, I didn't even know we were poor. I thought everyone lived like us. I thought all cheese came in a cardboard box. I didn't know what brand names were until nearly 6th grade. I was in fist fights nearly every single day simply because I didn't know how to fit in, so I tried to make myself fit. 4 different elementary schools in 6 years. Not off to a good start in life. Being the only Jewish kid at the schools I attended didn't exactly help. The 90s were tough for a Jewish kid in public schools in urban neighborhoods. After constantly getting the crap kicked out of me, (yes, I lost the first 200 or so fights in my life), I desperately needed to make a change or things were somehow going to become much worse for me. And one day before Christmas, of all things, is where everything seemed to change. It was merely as if a switched had been flipped. From that day forward, my life would never be the same.

Chapter 2

My family originates from Israel. I was born in Las Vegas, Nevada in February of 1983. A great portion of my childhood was spent in Sacramento, California. You don't realize that you're the child of an immigrant until someone manages to point it out. Nothing comes easy for someone who is always considered an outsider, or someone who has packed up their entire life and travelled halfway around the world to a country unknown to them to simply provide a better future for themselves and their children. But I found my niche. I found my way in and I found the one thing I'd soon excel in more than anything else. Only I wouldn't know it until many, many years later. Early on I realized I didn't need school, like you hear many children say. Only this was different. It's not that I disliked it, which of course I dreaded every moment of it. But I was so far ahead of my class, at times I'd get in trouble for simply correcting the teachers. And boy did they not like it one bit. How can you expect to succeed when the person teaching you has absolutely no clue what it is they are teaching you? You can't. It's a set-up for failure. So of course, I would do the required schoolwork, but I didn't pay much attention to anything my teachers ever said because moving forward in life is the goal, not being stuck working at a gas station when I turn 50.

The day before Christmas was the day everything changed. However, I wouldn't know it until a few days later. We had a tree in our front yard that was dying and needed to be cut down. My mother hired a tree service to cut it down. As an 11-year-old, watching these big with chain saws and ladders seemed pretty damn cool and somewhat dangerous, but I also knew this was more work than I'd ever care to do. When you know what you will and won't do, stick with it. I promise you can't go wrong sticking to your guns. After asking the tree trimmers why the tree needed to be cut down, they said it was dying. "How is it dying?", I asked. They said it was being suffocated by what was growing on it. The green little saplings that were growing on it looked oddly familiar. I'd seen this stuff around the holidays and had even seen people standing underneath it kissing one another. It was more popularly known as mistletoe. I knew people purchased this sort of thing. I immediately asked the tree trimmers if they could cut it down and separate it from the remainder of the tree. They kindly did so. I fled to the grocery store where I collected as many grocery bags as possible without someone noticing and returned home. After bagging up all the mistletoe I had, then using twist ties to seal the bags, I carried as many as I could going door to door selling them for $1 a bag. Increasing the price would've been a no brainer, but I had another idea in mind. Not only is $1 easy to part with for a child selling something on your doorstep, but its memorable. After selling about 30-40 bags, I was out of mistletoe and came home with a nice chunk of change. Not bad for an 11-year-old with a couple hours to spare. Zero overhead and 100% profit. Definitely can't go wrong there. That's when I learned what money was. And it was just the beginning. With no real clue of what I had just accomplished, I found a need and filled it with a product that people wanted. Of course, I didn't tell my mother who of course was working her butt off to support myself and my two sisters. And there's no way in hell I'm going to explain to my mother that I just made more money than her while working nearly a 1/3rd of the time she would need to, especially being 11 years old. For reasons I still can't explain, had she found out, she would beat the life out of me.

"Learning to save money when you've never had money and no financial training is incredibly difficult."

I had to hide my money and only spend it away from home. Never bring back something you clearly couldn't afford, because you'll have to answer for it, and I was not ready for that. I worked hard and wanted to keep what I had earned.

I soon realized that money was the key to changing my life. Some don't even realize this well into their 40's and 50's. Not only did I want to make money, I wanted to buy things, bring them home, and not get interrogated as to how I obtained it. So, a few months later my mom, my wonderful mother who came to this country not really understanding much of the American way, gave me an idea. It was an idea which inspired me to be creative and make some serious money at my age with both her knowledge and approval. However, what I was about to do, I don't think she had in mind or saw it coming. First, she gave me some speech about how when she was my age, she worked on a farm milking cows. I was now 12 years of age. There were no farms nearby and I'm pretty sure working was illegal in America at my age. After expressing my deepest apologies for what she endured as a child, I attempted to explain the many reasons why I couldn't obtain employment. Then again, she beat the crap out of me for being lazy and making excuses. Let me explain something. It was nearly impossible to refrain from laughing while my mom would beat me. Don't get me wrong, it hurt like hell. She in fact had served in the Israeli Military where nothing is funny and no one screws around. But my mother is no more than 5'3" – 5'4" and about 115 lbs. It's cute, but man does it piss her off when I start laughing. Of course, she'd often use a belt (buckle end first), or a high heel shoe like some Israeli assassin, and man was she accurate. I would never want to face my mother in a real fight. She's terrifying. But any regular ass whooping's are what kept me in line, and what caused me to be such a hard worker. I never gave up and to this day nothing has ever defeated me.

Chapter 3

I'm 12 years old and the proud owner of a fairly used lawnmower. My mother thought it would be a good idea for me to get out of the house and find some work. I could not have agreed more. She wanted for me to not be lazy. Besides, I needed the money. This was to be my next venture for success. With a couple of gas cans bungee corded to the lawn mower, a rake, some garbage bags, and not to mention my trusty clip board and pen, I began my journey through the neighborhood door to door. Doing this on the day that I planned on not cutting or raking a single yard was the goal. On this day I'd sign up as many people as possible so I would have scheduled days for money to regularly come in. To be honest, I mowed a few yards. Just enough to purchase a used weed whacker and second lawn mower. This way I could begin to tackle multiple jobs and thus increasing my income by charging for each additional service. Front yard and back yard, edged, raked and bagged, you're looking at roughly $25. Some folks I gave a discount to. But starting high allowed me to negotiate and maintain regular clients. After keeping pretty busy for a few months, my mother came home early one day and caught me sitting on the couch watching television. She asked why I wasn't working, when in fact I technically was. And keeping pretty busy I might add. So, I broke it down for her. And for some reason she was becoming angrier by the second. Explaining to her that I needed to be on the phone scheduling clients isn't what pissed her off. I think where she finally snapped was at the part where I explained I now had employees. One would mow, move on to the next yard, while the second would begin edging right behind and move on to the following yard, and finally one would bag everything up. I had a 60/40 split going and divided everything accordingly to whom did what job and how long it took them. To be completely transparent, I took the 40% and divided the remaining amongst the employees. They got to keep 100% of their tips and divide them evenly. They were actually very happy. And believe me, so was I. In just a few months, I must have made what some people make working in a year. That's when the next ass whooping ensued. As she was beating me, she attempted to explain the reason for me to work was to do the manual labor myself and to experience the difficulties that life would throw at me with its many challenges. I guess skipping right to becoming a CEO was not what she had in mind. During the process of her whooping me, while laughing hysterically due to some nervous tick, it sounded like a rap song. Half in Hebrew and half in English as she was running out of breath from the ass whooping. Man, my mom is tough. Needless to say, it was a pretty successful venture while it lasted. And again, it was marketing that helped it become such a success. I knew what the people needed, and I gave them a solution to the problem they had, while providing exceptional service.

By this point I had taken some of my money, bought new shirts, some new shoes that did not come from goodwill and soon realized girls were paying attention to me. I started having my older sister help me style my wavy and out of control hair. Then the money thing clicked in a new way. With money, I could look good, be presentable and attract the opposite sex. Well almost. I still had to get the whole delivery down when I spoke to them. Yet again, I learned all of it from sales and marketing.

"Remember, everything is a sale. It may come in different forms, but everything in life is a sale."

Sometimes you may end up on the buying end and other times on the selling end. Whether it's a product, service or simply meeting someone, it's all a sales pitch. If it looks good, it's unique, can spark conversation, someone somewhere is going to want it. Dress it up, make it loud, and put it out there. So that's exactly what I did.

Chapter 4

When you've had no kind of sales training and not much experience, you learn best from mistakes.

"Mistakes are not failures of any kind, they are just learning curves that over time you get better at approaching and navigating."

If not for my many learning curves in life, I would not be nearly as successful as I am. However, learning how to not let mistakes affect you is a big part of it. Some make mistakes and are quickly deterred from getting back up, moving forward, and trying again. Not me. To succeed is to overcome and to overcome means endless opportunities. And for me, endless opportunities mean endless amounts of money. Try it. You'll see.

One of the biggest mistakes I made early on was going big way too fast. Maybe not too fast, but sooner than I was ready for. I knew how to make decent money, but I wanted that suit and tie money, that seven-figure income money, my own mansion and a fleet of cars money, at the age of 12. Crazy, right? Nope. Determined. Often times, I would get on my bicycle and ride alone through neighborhoods where there was nothing but mansions. Some days I would ride for miles and for hours just to go look at these homes. I'd sit out front and wonder while gazing at these gargantuan homes, "What do these people do for a living?" I knew they weren't all professional athletes. Maybe some doctors, lawyers, or other high degree related positions, but I knew for a fact that a lot of them were business owners, entrepreneurs, and successful individuals who may have never set foot on a college campus other than to drop their kids off or pick them up. I was going to be one of those people. By 6th grade, I had skipped most 4th and 5th grade classes. School was too easy and not of any interest to me. College was never going to happen for me. No desire for it. I didn't want to be stuck at some stressful job working 20 hours a day dreading life. I wanted to be happy, successful, and help others. Be my own boss.

Chapter 5

Steps are crucial in life and I was quickly about to learn that I couldn't go from the first step to the top of the staircase in one leap. You can move up quickly, but you have still got to take it one or two steps at a time. Hanging out at bookstores is a good place to learn things. There are endless amounts of books on endless amounts of subjects. I figured that smart and successful people read, and boy was I right. Barnes & Noble wasn't too far away from my house. Roughly a seven to ten mile bike ride and I was at the mall. I would lock up my bike, go inside the massive book store in the parking lot of the mall, and begin to wander. At first, I learned the layout of the store. What types of books were where, and what kinds of people were into which ones. On the weekends, I'd often spend the entire day in the bookstore. I'd bring a snack or buy a drink and hang out. I read bits of all types of books. To a 12-year-old, Tony Robbins seemed like a cool guy. He inspired people, supported people and showed them how to achieve greatness in all aspects of life. I began paying attention to more and more of the people who come in to the bookstore. Soon, I was seeing what kinds of cars they were driving. I found a magazine that sold high end cars and exotic boats that seemed like no one could possibly afford. Hooked I was! Then, I started noticing cars in the parking lot with the same price tags as in the magazines. Those were the people I needed to talk to. Find out what they do for a living because clearly, they were doing something right. My sister, who is much older than I, owns a few businesses and also has her Master's

Degree in business once told me something. It was the best piece of advice she could have ever dropped on me,

"Hang around 9 successful people, and you will be the 10ᵗʰ. Hang around 9 broke people and you will be the 10ᵗʰ."

To this day I have never forgotten this.

"If you are happy with your miserable, crappy life, living paycheck to paycheck, barely getting by, riding the bus and have no care about improving your life, then you are just taking up space in front of me and I need to maneuver around you."

It's not about envy or greed. Let me make that perfectly clear. I'm glad you have nice shit. I don't want what you have. I'm after success. My own success. My own type of cool shit.

While at Barnes & Noble one day, I spotted a gentleman in a red Ferrari. He got out of it with a grey suit and matching red tie. It's like the tie said, "I came with the Ferrari." In this case, the car went with the tie, not the other way around. That same year, the film "The Rock" starring Nicholas Cage and Sean Connery was released and the only thing I remember was a bright yellow Ferrari chase from the entire film. Everyone remembers a Ferrari. It's a stand-alone symbol that screams, "I am successful." Back to Barnes & Noble. So, after watching this gentleman walk into the store, I kept my distance. He had on some expensive shoes, a nice watch, and what I found out later to be cuff links. Why would someone care about cuff links? A part of an outfit that serve absolutely no purpose and are hardly seen? It's because when they are seen, it sets a tone. The smallest things can make the biggest difference. Sure enough, after he grabbed a coffee he headed to the section of magazines and picked up the one I had been looking at. A DuPont

Magazine. Expensive cars and boats. He sat down and began reading it. He wasn't just looking at the cars, like someone in awe. He was looking like someone who might be a making a purchase. So, I approached him, told him my name and who I was. My first question was, "What do you do for a living?" He immediately realized I wasn't just an ordinary twelve-year-old. He handed me his business card and explained that he places high end vehicles in major motion pictures. You mean to tell me there a job where you put nice cars in movies? What else was I missing out on life? You can make a buttload of money by putting cars in movies. He then went on to explain that he owns a company that also constructs replicas of exotic cars to be purposely crashed in movies. That gave me a sigh of relief. All these years, I'd cringed thinking what a waste of a perfectly good car. Now when I see a high-end vehicle get smashed up in a movie, I go, "It's a fake car." I told him about my recent ventures and that I was dedicated to being successful due to wanting a similar lifestyle. He said to email him and that he would send me some info on what he does. So, I did. About 3 weeks later a package came in the mail for me. It was a fairly large package with pictures, info, and complete breakdowns of what his company did and was responsible for. On top of it, the cost and profit margins on provided services. This information was definitely helpful later in life. However, at the moment, a bit out of my league. Because there was just no way in hell that anyone was going to listen to anything a twelve-year-old was saying regarding anything costing $250,000 or more. It just wasn't realistic at the moment. A bit of a learning curve, not a failure. It opened my eyes though to a whole new level of marketing. A different group of potential buyers. People who made more money also spent more on purchases. Wealthy people don't buy cheap shit. It's just the way it is. As I learned more about pricier items, I started to meet people in bigger industries.

At the time pagers and flip phones were all the rage. I started meeting people who owned pager stores and cell phone stores. At the time, those were very popular big-ticket items. If I could get my hands on these, I could make some serious money. Junior High School came, and it was 1996. Recently, I'd made a solid contact at a local pager store.

I was able to get my hands on refurbished pagers in all colors and even an opportunity to get some really cool analog (yes, pre-touch screen phones. The ones that flipped open with a retractable antenna) phones and got them activated. I was now able to provide a product and sell it to kids in high school, who could not obtain these items for a low price. Plus, no credit check or personal information made it even more appealing to a lot of them. Soon, I had no room for books in my back pack. It was full of nothing but pagers and cell phones. This was the next logical step in moving up. Not straight to high end exotic cars. In the 90s, if you had a job paying $500-$600/week you were doing pretty well. I was clearing over $1,000/week. I became the kid everyone wanted to know. I went from the outcast, to the independent guy on a very positive level. Soon, I was being contacted by kids at other schools and going to parties. College parties! At 14 years of age, I was going to college parties regularly. My marketing skills were so on point, it was sick. Pretty soon, I was talking to more than 3 new girls each week. Money brings you everything!

Chapter 6

Now, I know exactly what you're thinking. This is borderline crazy. How is he doing this? And how on earth does his mother not know what's going on? Well, to answer your question, she might learn English, read this book, and pop up on a surprise visit and beat me within an inch of my life with this very copy. But hey, I'm going to spill it. Every last fucking drop. Not only did I have to hide my clothes and shoes because I was back to making money in a way my mother would never approve of. Granted, I was not selling drugs or stealing, but according to her I may as well have been. I got caught being outside late one night and my mother thought I somehow walked out the back door without her hearing it. She could somehow hear me whisper on the other end of the house at 2 A.M. I had no idea how good her military training was. So, one day she got this bright idea to put an alarm on the house. Not for intruders, but to keep me from sneaking out at night. That plan failed miserably. Not the alarm, in fact, ADT was and is still great. But, I quickly learned how to bypass the alarm while it was armed. Ever play with magnets growing up? I did. Because we were poor and those became toys for me. They work and I got really good at using them to bypass all the sensors in the house. I was back out partying in no time.

The concept of saving money at this moment in life eluded me. The concept of making it was another story entirely. And when I did spend, I spent like I was the king of Monaco. I started showing up to

14

random parties with friends. Parties we weren't even invited to, where not a single soul knew who we were. When you walk into someone's home uninvited, people quickly notice. Especially when not a single person has a clue as to who you or your guest is. But, when you track down a college party and show up unannounced and moments later a stack of pizzas arrives, along with bottles of liquor that you, yourself paid for, everyone's attitude changes quickly. Now you have more questions. At 15 years of age, how did I get pizza and alcohol delivered? Now you're asking the right sales questions. I made friends with a lot of the local pizza delivery guys to the point where I could call a location and request a specific driver. And because I always tipped VERY well, (sometimes $100 tip on a $15 order) they made themselves available when another potentially big tip was coming their way. A lot of pizza delivery drivers are roughly 21-24 years of age. They had bills to pay, gas, insurance, etc. So, I found people who needed the extra money. Not only would they bring the twenty-pizza order, but they would also show up at times with the requested fifteen to twenty bottles of liquor. Go ahead, add it up really quick. If you got to about a $500 order then you were just about spot on. Do you know what a customary tip was in the 90s? At minimum its 15% of the total bill. So, $75 would have been fair. To be honest, some people don't even tip the 8% tax when they dine out. Cheap ass people. But not me. I like to keep people available. If I couldn't get the pizza guy to stay and hang out then I'd tip him nearly 20%. If I could somehow talk him into staying and calling in some sort of emergency so he didn't have to return to work, (which meant stay, party with hot college chicks, and get free booze and pizza) then just for the hell of it, I would tip him double. Sometimes a $300 tip isn't so bad. It's what some made in tips in a week. He had fun, made good money, and I now had someone available to deliver items as needed. It's a win-win situation. That's what we call an independent contractor. Someone who is not on payroll that you keep around and pay for services as needed.

Things were going great. I was going to the movies with different girlfriends weekly. I even met a stripper who I convinced to let me drive

15

her car to school even though I didn't have a driver's license. My mother would not allow me to have a driver's license yet. But everything was better than ever. I've often heard;

"All good things must come to an end."

Not sure who came up with this saying, but it sounds like this guy fucked up bad. Why would someone be so negative to where that's a life saying? In my world, nothing comes to an end if you don't want it to. We get on and ride until the wheels fall off, then we grab another set and keep on rolling. Moderation was not something I was familiar with at the time. We didn't grow up moderately poor. We were broke as fuck and had been for generations. There was nothing moderate about it. This term caught up with me Sophomore year of high school. In sales and marketing, you have what are called trends. Knowing when something is going to be hot and knowing ahead of time when something is going to burn out. Meaning, get in while it's good and get out before disaster happens. This doesn't always happen to everyone, just know that it does happen quite often though. To the stock market, the real estate industry, hell, even the entire economy crashes at times. My time was also fast approaching. How long could I keep proving people with pagers and cell phones? For the time being, because it was hot, a lot of money came in quick. It was bound to plateau and slow down, but I never got to that point. One day, I came to school yet again with a backpack full of new pagers and cell phones. It was a good day. I remember getting through the first few classes with no issues. Then, suddenly I got this weird feeling in my stomach, like something wasn't right. It wasn't. I got called to the Dean's office. I had not a clue as to what I was about to walk into. Upon arriving to the office, another student who just purchased a phone from me the day before was also there. He wouldn't make eye contact with me and immediately, I knew what happened. I quickly ducked out of the office, headed back to the classroom and explained that I forgot my backpack (full of pagers and cell phones). I was about to get in

16

trouble. At the time, phones and pagers were not allowed at school in any capacity whatsoever. I ditched my bag in a safe location and headed back to the office. I was right. The student who was there got busted for his phone and ratted on me. Said I sold it to him and that I was selling them to everyone. Let's hope he never ends up in prison. Needless to say, I had no phones or pagers in my possession. When asked about my backpack, I said that I was running late that day and forgotten it at home. Bullet dodged.

That night at home, my mother got a hold of my backpack to check my homework and was quite surprised to find my surplus of phones and pagers. Let the beatings begin! Just kidding. By 16, I was nearly 6ft tall and she just smacked me around a bit. I deserved it. Needless to say, end of communications. All sales are final, no refunds, and going out of business. Mom single handedly shut me down.

"Losing a customer is sometimes worth it. They may think you owe them something, but you do not. Customers are a dime a dozen. They are not friends, so there is no love lost. Especially if it's a headache customer. Lose one and gain 10. Simply avoid the headache of tending to one problem and replace it with more solutions. Business 101. Know your customer base. If one customer becomes a complainer, then refund them. One complaint will always lead to more. It's not what you are doing wrong, it's just their personality type. The one who writes bad reviews, or badmouths someone to everyone. You can't please everyone, so don't even sweat it."

When one business closes, you can always move on to another. So, what do you think I did? I moved on and moved up. Next step!

Chapter 7

With all the money I still had from previous sales, I quickly picked up some catalogs and checked out some new electronics fresh out on the market. At this point in high school, car shows were popular. We were going to street races and it was a lot of fun. This was better than any party I'd been to. Remember the very first Fast & Furious movie? It was just like that, except real. And the adrenaline rush running from the cops was intense. I began going to street races almost every weekend. I knew a lot of the people from previous parties, got plugged into an entirely different network, and introduced to quite a few new ones. The smell of burning rubber mixed with girls wearing next to nothing, what more could a high schooler want? I still didn't have a driver's license, so buying an import and racing it out just to have it towed was out of the question. Besides, I got rides from friends. And if they couldn't give me a ride, often times I'd borrow their car. For the time being, that was more than enough for me.

People were just starting to put television screens in their cars. One in each headrest (including the very rear headrest so the cars behind them could see, we called this "hater vision"), with a detached head unit often times mounted under the seat. The in-dash models hadn't quite dropped yet. This gave me yet another great idea! While flipping through a magazine one night, I spotted a sale for two screens and the DVD head unit as a package and got the urge to call immediately. So, first thing the following morning I called with one specific goal in mind. To find out if they were wholesaler or just an authorized dealer of sorts. Turns out, it was even better than expected.

"Never pay full price when you don't have to. Buy low, sell high. Make sure your profit margins are as great as can be. If your profit margin is less than 30% on any retail item, walk the fuck away now."

I made my way through the company directory until I worked my way up to the voicemails of those who make the actual decisions. So, just to break it down, there was no listing of what extension to dial. I called about 30-40 times and when I figured out how many numbers were in the extensions and what they started with, I just kept trying over and over as each voicemail that picked up stated the person's name and their position with the company. The next day, I got a call back and asked to speak with the head of their sales department. Now, this company was located in the bay area and at the time I was living in Sacramento, CA. A two and half-hour drive wasn't too bad for what I was about to pull off. The sales guy for this company thought I was opening a new shop and wanted to purchase several units to resell at my location. Well, most of it was true. I was looking to purchase several units. I was looking to resell them. But what he didn't know is that I had no store and I was 16 years of age. He was in for a shock when I showed up two weeks later with a pocket full of money. You should've seen the look on his face when I walked in and explained to him that I'd been the person he was speaking with. At first, he didn't believe it. Then I pulled out my money. Well, some of it. Just enough to show I wasn't messing around. His attitude changed almost immediately. Pretty sure he was still trying to process what happened and how he somehow failed to realize he'd been discussing business with a sixteen-year-old.

At the time, two DVD screens and the head unit retailed for $749.99. I was told if I bought 3-5 complete units then my price would drop to $399.99 for each unit. Not a bad bargain, right? A 75% margin is incredibly rare. So, I took it a step further. I asked him how many units he had currently available to sell. He told me he had about 20 complete units at the moment. I told him I would take all 20 units if he would drop the prices to $349.99 per unit. He immediately said no. I then proceeded to pull out most of the remaining money I had brought with me, just to show him how serious I was. Then I turned around and began to walk out of the store. Right as I reached the door, he shouted out behind me, "Fine! I'll do the 20 units for $349.99 each." I smiled and then turned back around towards him. Not only was he now doing exactly what I wanted, but for thinking I was a fool, he was about to have another thing coming.

"In sales, you have to know your audience. Get them right where you want them and then flip the script. Make it to where they now NEED you and not the other way around. They want to make the sale. In fact, a lot of the time they NEED to. A company or supplier is not in the market of keeping product. Their sole job is to get rid of it as soon as possible."

So, I decided to knock him out with my best marketing tool. My mouth. I then asked, "When is the next shipment expected to come in?" He told me it would be the following week.

"A company loves nothing more than to have items and services pre-sold. To sell something you don't have in your possession or haven't completed yet is ideal. It means there is guaranteed revenue coming in. Scheduling revenue to come in is much easier than chasing the dollar each day. Facts!"

I told him to pull 20 more units aside for me. He was a bit shocked. He thought I was kidding. I said, "Fine, then I won't buy anything." This time, I made it clear out to the car winging an entirely different plan. Before I got into the car, the thought of losing all those sales must have sunk in. So, this is exactly what I told him was going to happen next. Not only was I leaving with the 20 units today, but I was not paying $349.99 a piece either. I was paying $299.99 each and putting a cash down payment towards the next order. See what I did? The money I was going to spend anyways on the current units, I diverted. I took the same money that was going to be spent and used it to put it towards the next order. Didn't lose a single cent. If all was lost and this deal didn't go the way I intended, then I would have only been out the money I initially intended to spend regardless. By doing this, I got the units cheaper and reserved a bunch more that I would now pre-sell the moment I got back home. This doesn't happen all the time. But you need to stand your ground and show how serious you are regarding every single business encounter.

"If you can show that it benefits everyone involved, chances are you will walk away with exactly what you want."

So, there I was, heading back home with a trunk full of product and he had a bag full of money. My profit margins just increased exponentially. Just to move all of the new units as quickly as possible. As soon as I got back home, I went to every single person I knew who was working on their vehicles for upcoming car shows. I sold all 20 units in less than a week for only $700 each. I gave everyone a deal just so they'd refer me for the next shipment I was about to receive. And yes, although I sold them for slightly less than anticipated, I also paid less than expected. My cost was $299.99 and I sold them for $700 each. That's nearly a 130% profit margin. As I love to say, winning! And when I pre-sold the next 20 units scheduled to come in, I had each client put half down on them out of trust and reliability. Having each person put half down ensured that all of my costs would be covered upon the shipment's arrival, meaning I then would owe my distributor absolutely nothing. Can you say winning, again? I profited nearly $16,000 in two weeks. Holy shit! Not half bad for a sixteen-year-old. After paying my ride back and forth to pick up everything, along with some bills I accumulated along the way, I walked away with just over $14,000. That's when I got really hungry. Not for lunch, but for something even greater than I ever imagined. I did extremely well for quite a few months. Then these things got so popular that every store in the area started carrying them and that began to saturate things. At the time I wasn't really aware of what was happening, but I soon realized it. I could sell anything to anyone! I taught myself the ins and out of marketing before I even really knew what marketing was.

Chapter 8

I turned 17 and finally got my driver's license. Bought a new car very carefully. I told my mom that I had earned enough for a down payment and had her write the check for $2,500 down on my new Pontiac Sunfire GT. What an amazing piece of crap that car was. But, at the time I didn't know this. All I knew was that I had a new car and could go on even more dates now. My mom was somehow led to believe that I had a part time job, but I was using my savings to pay my car payments. I was now burning through money like my pockets were literally on fire. And no, I still did not have a new business opportunity at hand. Man was I screwed. On the verge of being broke, what do I do? Here's another good rule of thumb when working on your own business throughout your life.

"Keeping past client info is always a smart move. You may come across new opportunities and need to reach out to gain support and sales."

One evening I was driving home in my new Pontiac Sunfire GT. It was raining. I was thinking about a new business opportunity, when out of nowhere a ¾ ton pick-up truck ran a stop sign and t-boned my fiberglass 2 door sports car. I was fucked. The truck took off, and by the time I came to, the fire department was cutting me out of what was left of this car. I learned a very crucial thing that week. When it comes to business and life in general, always, always, always, cover your ass.

Anything and everything that can go wrong, at some point in life will go wrong. At the time, I had no health insurance. My hospital bill, ambulance bill and medication payment wiped me completely out. I went broke almost instantly. Like broke broke. My car was totaled. The insurance I had at the time only covered the actual value of the vehicle, not the entire loan itself. I missed a little thing called GAP insurance, which at the time would've helped tremendously. Meaning that if you somehow owed more than what the vehicle was worth, this added insurance would cover the remaining balance. Now I had no money, no car, and I was injured on top of that. Had I not been injured, my mother for sure would've injured me. For someone who knows how to hustle, I sure got hustled bad. Then things went from bad to worse. I healed up, got my girlfriend at the time pregnant and joined the Marine Corps. Clearly, I had no clue what I was doing. I was grasping at straws at this point. The marketing guru was shaken and I didn't know if I'd be able to recover from what just happened.

Chapter 9

At seventeen years of age, I joined the Marine Corps. The best decision my mother ever made for me. She was tired of me feeling sorry for myself after my injury and sitting on the couch nearly every day. It truly was the best decision ever. Only thing was that I didn't know what 9/11 was about to bring. When you know something devastating is going to happen nearly two weeks prior to it happening, and you can't do anything about it, it's horrible. And something you will never forget. For legal reasons and the fact that I'd like to remain a somewhat free person in this country, I cannot divulge information that led up to that tragic day in 2001. All I can say is that nearly my entire unit was killed overseas, and luck was on my side. I happened to be somewhere else, nowhere near the middle east, doing something completely different, but as equally important. Or so I was told it was.

I came home a while later, to a beautiful baby boy and a much stronger mindset than I had left with. Things were going to get better and there was no other option.

I share this with you for one reason.

"Everyone will fall down at one point or another in their life. It's not about getting back up that's important, it's how you get back up."

We all have the ability to get back up. But how we do it, is a whole different story. Your brain is a muscle and therefore, you must work it out regularly. Just like muscles in the gym. You lift, they get stronger. I did a lot of psychological training and improved quite a bit. From this point forward, nothing was going to stop me ever again. I am a machine. Little did I know, I was about to take marketing to a whole new level.

My body and mind were in the best shape ever at this time. However, I had been out of sales and marketing for some time while being away. My confidence level sky rocketed, so speaking to people became much more natural. I somehow radiated confidence everywhere I went. My positivity levels were much higher, I engaged with more people, and I was more aware of my surroundings on several different levels. By the time I left the Marine Corps, I had been trained on security and surveillance to a point that was just beyond ridiculous. So naturally, I went into the security field. I now had to sell myself. This part was entirely new to me. I'd always been able to sell products, but I had never once consciously thought about how to actually market myself. So, I went to a close friend at the time who was dating rappers and pro athletes. She told some of them her good friend is a trained Marine and available for private security if needed. My life took a sudden turn that I never saw coming. I was now the product being marketed. I had to package myself properly and present myself in a way so that I conveyed to someone who was not in security, that I knew exactly what I was doing. To make someone feel they could be safe secure. Being around celebrities was a whole new world for me. You can't get excited. Well, you can, you just can't show it on the outside. You must remain professional at all times and never ever ask for autographs or photos unless they offer. Even then, it's polite and professional to decline. And sometimes it's hard, because there are times you may be working for someone that you are actually a huge fan of. The key is discipline. Discipline can take you to places you can only dream of. The more discipline you have, the more successful you will be. For a span of roughly nine years, I did celebrity executive protection. I went from working for some of the craziest rappers ever, to some of the biggest and most respected athletes and celebrities on the planet. How did I do it? Marketing!

I never worked for a company, and was always referred personally. Marketing comes in various forms. Want people to listen to you? Get their attention. Get them to like you. Give them a reason to listen. Like a famous actor once said,

"If you're good at something, never do it for free."

Often, I was with celebrities while they handled business or conducting some new endorsement deal. A lot of the time, it was during family vacations that I was spending time with them. I got the chance to see both sides to these amazing and incredibly successful people. How they handled things on the personal side of their life, which could both make and break their careers, and how they did it professionally.

"Learning how to read people is a huge key in marketing. Figuring out what they want before they even realize it themselves, that's exceptionally good marketing."

If you complain, don't do it in public. If you own a business or a provide a service, never show any type of emotion in public unless it exhumes happiness and appreciation. All it takes is one negative vibe to be seen and passed along. That can cause people to avoid you or never purchase from you again. Marketing includes your appearance, your attitude and your interaction with others.

Speaking your mind and not being afraid of what others think, should terrify you if you own a business. By all means, if you are an advocate of free speech, not worried about your income and don't have any bills to ever worry about, or if you're a stand-up comic, then let it flow. Say whatever comes to your mind. But if you are a business owner, then shut the fuck up! Watch what you say and learn how to market your mouth.

Throughout the years of doing executive protection, and being a single father, I would often spend time at the gun range. In fact, without really realizing it, there were weeks I would often find myself there anywhere from 3-4 times. With my Marine Corps training and knowledge of weapons, my proficiency level was through the roof. I hadn't engaged much with others due to my profession. However, people soon began to approach me on the ranges that I frequented. Sometimes to watch, or other times to make bets. Either way, taking their money and impressing them became this new exciting addition to my hobby. And it was like a switch flipped. Marketing was back!

Some would say I was little cocky, but when you're that good at something, I don't see it that way. My take on it was more confidence than anything. I started to make quite a few friends at the ranges and would often have shoot offs with random law enforcement officers and agents who would just be out shooting for the day. Imagine my surprise when one day a police officer approached me and asked if I had any tips for him. He could see how good I was just from my demeanor and the way I handled my weapons. Whenever I worked with any team, security or military, they were normally excited to have someone like me on board. I specialized in counter-surveillance. I took every job I did very serious. If I screwed up, then your favorite celebrity was in serious trouble. Thankfully, in the 9 years not one single time has a client ever been in danger. Never once did I have to draw my weapon while doing any executive protection detail. That's success. But I loved shooting. For me, it's very therapeutic. Yeah, you could go to some therapist and bitch and complain, go through all that bullshit, about feelings and emotions, and who knows what might happen. But this is guaranteed. Shooting drains all of your innermost thoughts, worries and physical stress. I've never had a better night sleep than the one after I had been shooting.

So, I began helping some police officers get better at their shooting techniques. Soon they were telling their law enforcement friends and before I knew it, I was hanging out with more federal agents, cops, and military personnel than I knew what to do with.

Chapter 10

At this point in my life, I began to draw up designs for new weapons. Not sure exactly where it came from, but I had the urge to do so, so I did it. And it was for no other reason than just for me. In the Marine Corps, I carried an M4, but it wasn't the most ideal size for every application such as being in a vehicle, breaching a home, or any sort of confined area. It just took up a tad bit more space than required. So, I wanted to develop and design something a little more practical for those types of situations. Something with just a bit more maneuverability while not losing any power. (I'm sure at this point in life you may be familiar with what's known as an AR-style pistol, or have been fortunate enough to see and or play with one. You may have possibly even had something similar in a caliber of 9mm, 40, or even .45 ACP that may or may not take a Glock magazine. Well, if you have, then you're very welcome. I single handedly made those compact weapons as popular as they are. I got them placed on LAPD motorcycles as well as other Law enforcement agencies. But before I get to all of that, let me explain how it started.)

I spent time sketching up ideas on napkins, then on paper. I studied the trajectory, as well as all math and science that would be required to adapt these specific weapons for close quarters combat use. I wanted a weapon that would exceed all expectations if needed for practical application. To be perfectly clear about something, I completely failed science and math at every stage in school except elementary school. I couldn't even begin to explain the chemical compounds and why on earth some genius thought we should put letters in math problems. Did I mention I fly airplanes and know absolutely jack fucking shit about geometry? There are just certain things I know, and have a thorough understanding of, in the most obscure ways.

With all my weapons drawings, a buddy of mine asked me what I was doing. I told him, "Dreaming." And then he asked me to explain. So, I did. When I was done, he laughed at me for nearly an hour. I asked, "What's so funny about wanting to develop military grade weapons so good that nothing has to be changed on them? Why can't I buy a weapon that comes fully upgraded as a factory model?" Meaning no trigger swaps, barrel swaps, or any upgrades after I took it home. He explained that it doesn't work like that. "It's a business. Guns, just like any other product are going to made with a primary base model. This is to keep profit margins at a certain point. It's just way too expensive to develop what you want, and have it sold as much as it needs to." All I heard was "challenge". A challenge I would soon put all my available time and effort into. Again, I was looking to develop one single weapon for myself that would beat all expectations.

How many times have you thought about a product that would be, or could be amazing? Have you written them down? Sketched it out? Once you do, everything changes. It's no longer just a thought. It's left your mind and onto paper. Now it's the first actual step to a tangible item in the real world. Now your options are only limited by your imagination. As a matter of fact, do it right now. I'll wait. Get a piece of paper and a pencil and quickly write down a list of inventions or business ideas you have been thinking about. It doesn't matter how crazy or simple it might be. Just do it. Take a solid minute then come right back and pick up at this very spot.

You know what you just did. You took the first step towards success. We'll get back to your list shortly. For now, save it. Something on that list is going to make you very successful one day. And guess what? When you do make it happen, you will need to market the hell out of it.

So, I told my friend that I was serious and he immediately saw that nothing on my face said I was joking. He quit laughing mid breath. "You're serious?" he asked. When you are serious about something just do it. Don't just say it. If you tell someone something, deliver. They'll never doubt you again. He saw just how serious I was and offered to help. Not because he wanted to be a part of it, but because he had just heard something so crazy that he had to see if it would really work. Intrigue someone with your pitch and watch how quickly they offer to help or point you in the right direction.

"Everyone wants to be involved in the next great thing."

Little did I know what he had in store for me. C and C machines can cut virtually anything into any shape, for any purpose. So, I learned really quick how to cut what needed to be cut in order to change the way we utilize and look at weapons today.

You might think, okay, who just decides to do something like this out of nowhere? Well first of all, it wasn't out of nowhere. It was needed. And second of all, that person is me. You want to be successful? Well stop talking, and start doing.

Chapter 11

It was a Sunday afternoon. I had just awoken. Suddenly out of nowhere I got this urge to fly an airplane. Two hours later I was at a flight school filling out paperwork and on my way down the runway for my first flight behind the yolk of a Cessna 173. If that's not enough, I'm a diehard NASCAR fan. I know and have even had the opportunity to work for one of the greatest drivers of all time. One day, I wanted to get behind the wheel of a stock car and I did it. People have always told me I live with my head up my ass or in the clouds. That life is not some big fantasy that I live in. Well, I'm sorry that your life is that damn horrible. And guess what? To all of you who say I am out of my mind, I am! And I'm incredibly successful at living out all my goals and dreams. Your dreams seem to be my reality. They can be yours too.

After designing a few personal AR-style weapons for myself, I began taking them out to the range to break them in and get them functioning properly. Again, this was strictly for my own personal weapon and not for any other reason. Just to see if it could be accomplished. During this process, I got new ideas for weapons development by watching law enforcement train and what they were dealing with on a daily basis. So, in turn, my weapon ideas were to improve upon their performance. To give them the upper hand. From the beginning, my idea was strictly from a military and law enforcement standpoint. I must have been onto something. One day while taking a break at the range, between training some law enforcement agents that I had been working with on tactical maneuvering, I began to test fire these weapons I had developed on my break. Nothing crazy. Just your standard .223/.556 ballistics on a very nice platform. One officer took notice. A very close notice and even asked if I could teach him how to shoot this new weapon he had not seen before. So, I did. It took some training as most are either used to shooting one of two ways. Either holding a handgun out in front of you or clutching a rifle to your shoulder. This was neither one of those common ways. This was a new style. A new application. A new everything. And everyone soon took notice. After this first officer got comfortable with this brand-new weapon, he told his partner about it and then he also wanted to try it out. Pretty soon, I was asked to bring it out every time we went shooting. So, I did. It was a big hit. Again, something I created and had an eye for, became an eye catcher. A conversation piece so to speak. Marketing! Marketing! Marketing! Now for the part I knew was bound to come. When someone sees something unique, that's uncommon, and no one they know has anything like it, they want it! And boy do they want it badly! Supply and demand folks. What I was doing without realizing it was testing the market. A market that this particular item was specifically designed for. Sometimes, you can base your price on how badly someone wants something. Drive the price up by immediately making that item no longer currently available. You can do this with almost any product. Try it. Next time someone asks you if you are selling a particular item, tell them you hadn't thought about selling it because it's something you were hoping to hang on to. They'll offer you a price and immediately decline it. And respond with something like, "If I were to ever consider selling this, I couldn't part with it for that price." Now you're in business. Counter with a number that's almost double. By the time they pay you, you'll have made at least 50%-70% more than you would've received had you just posted it and sold it. In my case, we were not there yet. These weapons were not available because they didn't really even exist. So therefore, I could not sell them. This instantly led to a frenzy of offers. If law enforcement wanted this item from me, then I knew I was onto something fantastic!

Chapter 12

If you plan on marketing something, always remember;

"Market the shit out of it! Don't try to sell a little of it. Sell the shit out of it! Oversell it! Sell so much you are on back order!"

If you can market like this, you'll never go broke again. Give people deals so good at first that even you get jealous. But limit it. Hook a few and strangle the rest.

With the right marketing, you can make something appear more valuable than it is. People pay $5,000-$20,000 for a dog because of exceptional marketing. Rapper 2 Chainz has a French Bulldog, so everyone wants one. By the way, in case you were wondering, you can get dogs virtually free on sites such as Craigslist. Think about it. Why is someone willing to pay so much money for a chore? Because someone made it look cool and very fashionable. Me? I'm never paying that much money for something that just shits and throws up everywhere.

"One plus one equals three. One for you, and two for me."

This business line is a simple math principle for marketing. It is one that I learned from an MBA holder. If you are doing business of any kind, keep this in mind. It's basic but very informative. And keep in mind with any business, I market and I have a product. You, the consumer or customer get the product or service and then I get paid from the sale. If you are doing business and barely breaking even then there is a huge problem. It's either your business model or most likely the way you're marketing. Remember singer Mark Morrison? "Return of the Mack" is quite literally one of the worst songs to have ever been recorded, yet it was. It might in fact be one of the worst songs of all time both musically and lyrically. But why and how is he still getting paid from this one song so many years later? Marketing! Incredibly, well-done marketing. If not for marketing he would quite possibly be working at a tire shop today. Instead, his song is all over television. Make it look good, and again, market the shit out of it!

Chapter 13

After a few months of refining my new weapons system, I started to get it down to where I was comfortable with it. Meaning someone with exceptional skills in the weapons world would use this exact set-up for real world defense and it would additionally exceed all my needs. It had to be lightweight, aesthetically pleasing, and above all else, perform better than anything else in comparison. It did just that. I wasn't just working on something cool at this point. I was making life altering developments. This could mean life or death for the person who would be trained on this weapon system, and my gamble was on them coming home sooner and safer. And I would guarantee it when the time came. The world is big on security. Guns are what a strong military relies on. Without quality weaponry, your country would be overtaken in a heartbeat. Guns are what win wars, protect lives, and ensure the freedoms our country advertises.

America is the biggest marketing campaign on the planet. We're constantly yelling "We're #1!" Who are we yelling at? Everyone that is not us. Everyone that is not us, wants to be us. Everyone that is not here, wants to be here. The flag, the way it waves in the wind, the fact that I can jump in my new muscle car and go to a nearby gas station to pick up an ice-cold bottle of water whenever I want, without hiking 10 miles with a bucket on my head, America! This place is a consumer's wet dream. Everything is available and EVERYTHING is for sale. Even if someone says it's not.

I started to showboat my new toys I had recently developed all over social media. If you know how to advertise through social media the way I know how, you'd be wealthy. But you don't, so I'll help you. I'm quite literally the King of social media marketing. Can you take or create a product in a really niche market, and then turn it into a company grossing over $100 million? If not, don't worry because I can, thanks to social media and my unique set of skills.

"I can take your business and generate up to an extra six figures annually. No billboards. No magazine articles. No television commercials. No flyers. No shit. I'm that damn good. In fact, over the years, all of the celebrities and businesses I have worked with like Fox and ESPN are more than enough to prove that."

I began getting so many messages about my new weapons system that there was almost no way to keep up. This is where I had to make a life altering decision. What was my endgame with this product? Funny that the word endgame came to mind, because right as this question entered my mind, I was watching Iron Man. To be more specific, Tony Stark. And that's the moment I knew exactly what I was going to do. I was going to be a Defense Contractor. The biggest and baddest one there was. I had so many weapon development ideas that the government was going to love it. And more importantly, so was my pocket book.

Here's the problem, more like the starting point. There is only a problem if you have no solution. For one, I do not do anything that I cannot do well. I had one weapon developed. No business. No nothing. But why is this also a perfect problem to have? Because now it's time to figure out how to build and grow. Everything starts with a seed. An idea if you will. You plant it, water it, take care of it, and then make every fucking dollar possible from it!

I made a list of everything I would need to begin legally creating weapons for the government. Since I decided Defense Contractor was my goal, there was a shit ton of paperwork to be done. Which I knew absolutely jack shit about at the time. So, after enlisting some help from a few government employees and several meetings later, my paperwork was being completed. A warehouse was allocated, machines were utilized and before I knew it, I had nearly 6 different types of military weapons available. Now, you might be wondering how much money all of this would cost. Well, what if I told you that I started with only $45,000 from my own pocket, and within four years was looking at grossing well over $100 million annually? Not bad, huh? Not bad at all.

A key piece of successful business is knowing when and where to make sacrifices. In my case, to become a successful government contractor, I would have to low-ball a contract so low that I felt like I took a serious shot to the nuts. You know, the kind that hits you just right and knocks the wind out of you while sending that shooting pain into your lower abdominal region? That low. And why would any business person do such a thing? For one simple reason. Nothing other than to just acquire that contract so someone else couldn't. You get a good one no matter what, you'll make some serious money because of it. You use it as leverage. And leverage is key.

"In order to bring in some serious money, sometimes you need to strategize the long game."

Things were going well from day one and I couldn't have been happier. I was soon being introduced to everyone as their "gun guy" or, "This is my friend, he's an Israeli arms dealer." Not going to lie, it sounded cool as shit. Especially during the week of the Mayweather vs. McGregor boxing match. Every time I was introduced to someone, Mayweather would say, "This is my gun guy." Not saying I provided the Champ with anything, but just introducing who I was in a friendly nature.

"There's a difference between owning a gun store and designing weapons. It's like being Georgio Armani or the guy who just wears an Armani knock off suit."

Chapter 14

With social media, it's like 5 o'clock rush hour on the 405 freeway in Southern California. All day long, bumper to bumper traffic. People posting ads everywhere. It's actually quite unbelievable if you think about how many items and services are being posted every second around the world.

My goal now after the development of my weapons system was to advertise it to the mass public. Why? Because everyone wants something they can't have. Exclusivity. And now that I was working on something for a specific military and law enforcement application, I knew something was going to catch on in a big way. I designed a new logo and hit the streets running, so to speak. Now armed with extensive knowledge of how to locate everyone on social media who was into firearms, and any sort of niche thing I had developed, I linked a Twitter, Facebook, and Instagram account all together and targeted a mass audience. Within one month, I had nearly 100,000 followers and interests were building. Questions were being asked, and message after message was flooding all of my inboxes.

If you have something everyone is interested in, yet for some reason you cannot provide them with this product or service, you do the next best thing. Create a product or service that they can have which resembles that which they cannot actually acquire. Merchandise. Loads and loads of retail items with the logo of the exclusive items that are not available. People may not be able to obtain certain items, but they will wear something with that logo on it. Don't believe me? Take a look around.

One of the first people ever to reach out to me was a professional bodybuilder. He explained that he was a convicted felon, could not be around any firearms, but loved what the company brand stood for. Our creed. Our motto. What it represented to each individual. That you were the best of the best.

"I work hard. I never give up. Every day I give 110%. There are no limits to my capabilities. There is nothing I can't achieve. I conquer and dominate all I do. I have no bar. I have no ceilings. I break through barriers. I am unstoppable. I am a King Assassin."

And that's how he felt in the gym and therefore wanted a t-shirt to work out in with our logo on it. Because you are the best at what you do, you are #1, you want others to know it, to be encouraged by it, and to know they can do it also. Again, welcome to America.

So, we had some really nice shirts designed and sold out of them almost immediately. Before I knew it, I was on the phone with one of the largest condom manufacturers around. A representative of theirs had contacted me through Instagram and pitched to me. He started with, "You guys make things for self-defense and protection, and so do we. We are interested in creating a line of condoms with your logo on it since your brand is growing so quickly." I wanted to know the money details. Once that was figured out, I was in. Before I knew it, we had high end coffee cups and custom shot glasses that resembled cylinders from old Colt revolvers, which came in these really nice handmade boxes going for nearly $250 for a set of 4. And just when I thought it couldn't get any better, I'm doing a phone conference with Mechanix. The most popular glove company on the planet is talking to me about our own line of gloves through their line. Co-branding and marketing at its finest. These gloves are both seen and used by virtually every mechanic out there, from your do-it-at-home mechanic to NASCAR crews. I was in immediately. My brand was now growing exponentially. And who did I end up meeting with shortly after? A skateboard team from NIKE and people who are doing sports videos for Red Bull. So now we are looking into making skateboard decks, snowboards and possibly surfboards.

After a well-known Pro-MMA fighter, whom I won't mention, but his last name rhymes with Diaz, had our logo on his shorts one night during a fight on television, things grew even more. My brand is now getting into professional sports. I'm gaining traction on things I never imagined. All because of some amazing marketing. Like I said before, I know what I am doing and I am doing it well. I don't pick up every offer that comes my way, but the smart ones you don't pass up. How do you know which offers those might be? By reading the market. What are people into? What do they like? And what are they typically buying?

Everyone has their particular brand that they buy specific things from. Beer, makeup, cell phones, and cars are just a few examples of what people purchase to a dedicated point. So, you then get into things that are universal where someone will pick the same item up from, but through a different brand. For instance, people buy t-shirts from everyone everywhere. Concerts, stores, and all different types of locations. Hats, bracelets, shot glasses, and other retail items they can have multiples of. I even ventured into a line of beer mugs. Yes, they did very well. Almost anything I threw my logo on moved like it was on fire. Building that foundational support for your business not only ensures sales, but future sales as well. You want the same person who just bought something from you to stick around, and come back to buy other stuff. We call these repeat clients or customers.

It soon got to a point where nearly 90% of my products were now retail items. Guns were specifically for one market, while the brand itself was burning up another. Hats came next. This even surprised me. The company, whom you see in nearly every mall across America, wanted to do our hats. This was a market that was untouched for my brand. The younger generation. Of course, the younger crows should be empowered and want to be the best at what they do. So, I wanted them to look that way as well. Now we are moving high end fitted baseball hats with our logo puffed out on the front. What market have I not touched? The baby market was next. Just not yet. We weren't quite there.

Chapter 15

Instant gratification and trends are what make sales. How so? Make someone feel great by having your product and they will continue to buy from you. Then it creates a trend. "I feel good because I have" or, "I'm using" statements help your product create increased sales. How? When someone has those thoughts or feelings and shares them with other people, it eases the minds of those who may be interested in it as well. When one sees someone else with it or using it, they themselves feel the urge to as well.

Want even more marketing? Good. Because I'm not even close to the end. Buckle up and hang on. Speaking of buckle up. I'm kidding. We don't have a line of seatbelts, but we should!

A particularly large summer was fast approaching for a specific "sport". I use sport in quotes, because what I am about to talk about, in no way shape or form did I know this was a sport. It seemed more of an aggressive workout. Had this very much in shape young lady not talked me into this "sport" and explaining its rich history and that it was in fact a sport, a major part of our apparel line would not even exist. Normally, if I hear something and I am not interested I am done with it. There's nothing you can do or say to convince me about something I have no interest in. It just doesn't work. Unlike most people, no matter how convincing or amazing the sales person might be, I am not budging. No amount of discount, or free shit or whatever else you attempt to do to "sweeten" the deal is going to work. Sweeten is a word us business people use. It means "to add sugar to". I'm kidding, I know you know what it means. But, I am just not that guy. When it comes to business, I stay focused.

However, show me I can make money off of whatever you're talking about and all of what I just said goes right out the window. I know, right? Just because I may not be interested, doesn't mean that millions of other people are not. And if I am curious to see if this is in fact true, there's a way to test the theory. To be quite honest, I don't actually care what your business is. Not saying that it's irrelevant, I'm saying I have a formulated way to find people who are interested in what you have or do regardless of what it is. Interested enough to stick around and quite possibly become customers and even return customers. Even if your products are made from recycled underwear. I am definitely not your demographic; however, I know who is. It's true. If there is a market that exists for your product or service, I will find it.

"That's what the King of Marketing does. Anyone can take pictures and pay for advertisements, but I go direct to the people who are already interested in what you have, bypassing all the extra spending and wasted time that is incredibly valuable to your business and revenue."

Now back to this "sport". When she told me that rowing was a sport, I almost had my drink shooting out of my nose. This is not a fucking sport. I had to explain to her in great detail, that where I come from, rowing we pictured rowing as something rich white people did at their ivy league colleges for fun. Boy, was I immediately corrected. Although I was partially right, there was something else to this. Turns out, this is also an Olympic sport. Excuse me? Did you say Olympic sport? Yes. As in the Olympics we all watch on television. And that's exactly what she was talking about. She was in fact a professional rower. I needed more insight. Soon, I was looking at pictures of women who look like they could snap me in half. Holy shit! Can you say cha-ching! I asked her what the interest in my brand was. Her reply was one I already knew was coming. "Your brand represents individuals who give 110% everyday, no matter who they are. I want to be a part of that. I'm in the gym 5 days a week and on the water 3 days a week and I give my all to my craft 365 days a year." Now suddenly, I was motivated. I wanted to row a boat! Just kidding. I don't want to row shit. I wanted a boat, but like a regular boat, like a yacht. And by the way, these row boats are actually not called boats at all. This pissed her off but I quickly learned. She told me all of our products were targeted towards more of the male audience. As buff as she was, I don't know who she was fooling, but I soon saw her point. The only group I had not included into my brand were women and it was not intentional.

Now for some drastic decisions. Back to the drawing board. While I was working on a new logo for the female side of our brand, an NHL player reached out to me from the New York Islanders. He currently plays for the Redwings now. Not going to mention his name, but he stops the puck from going into the net. And his last name starts with a G and his first name starts with a T. No more clues.

This T.G. guy was interested in my brand. Big into firearms, big into working hard and definitely gives 110% on the ice from my research. Soon he was going to be wearing my stuff at practice. The NHL would not allow our brand on the ice during regular season play due to it being affiliated with firearms. Who cares? I still managed to attract their players individually. Which told me, if professional athletes are interested then I am definitely doing something right.

Is there an avenue I can't touch? I don't think so. I'll market your business and show you just how effective I am. My techniques are proven to work because you'll actually see the numbers growing right before you. It's like this. I bring you 50K followers to your social media page and you will see them. You will visually see them with your own two eyes, or one eye, depending on how many you have. And you will see on your Instagram, Facebook and Twitter pages all of the individuals that you know are supporting your business whom are both current and future clients. Sales are a number game and you want to do as well as you can in that game. The more clients, the more sales. To get these clients, I do some intensive and formulated direct client marketing, bringing them right to you. If I build a page for someone up to a million followers, their revenue increases by at least a minimum of up to $20,000 a month. That's without sales. The bigger your foundation, the more your business is seen. The more interaction you gain, the more money you make.

As I began making the finishing touches to the new female logo for our brand, something occurred to me. Women spend a lot of money. Of course, this is common knowledge, but in my business, women weren't a target market. In fact, no one except the government was our primary sales target. Now an entire line of products was formulating in my mind for the female population. Starting with the rower I spoke to. I introduced a line of high-quality athletic wear for her to review, use, tear up, and demolish as she saw fit. Not yoga pants who are worn by those who don't actually exercise. Those would come later. I gave our products to a real Olympic athlete to test out. I needed to know what she thought about the style, color, fit, comfortability and most important durability. She wasn't just jogging. She was enduring rigorous training that goes above and beyond what the average person does when they work out. Sure as shit, she was impressed. So, I picked out some solid power colors and got to work on mass producing this new female sportswear line. We sold out in the first week. Not just to athletes, but even locals who just wanted to feel great!

Don't be fooled. Retail is one of the toughest markets there is for a number of reasons. Mainly because it's so competitive, with thousands of companies for people to choose from. What made mine stand out was the brand itself. The brand stood for something, so anything I put that logo on, also meant it too was important.

Chapter 16

Bursting at the seams with all this new merchandise! If you get more than you can handle going on, things can start to not go as planned. To prevent that you must know when you're spreading yourself thin. If you need to, delegate. That's what I did. I can't even count how many people were developing my creations. At any given moment there must have been 5-10 new items in one week from different manufacturers for me to approve. On top of it all, we still had weapon designs being worked on. I'm at my peak pushing twenty-hour days without barely as much as a "hi" or "bye" to my son, whom at the time I was raising alone. Yes, I was doing all of this while raising a child by myself. I can't even begin to tell you how much support I was receiving due to this difficult period in my life.

I felt as though there was room to improve and work much harder. A lot was on my mind. As the female sportswear line was developing and flying off the shelves, I was next contacted by a small wine club. What's a wine club? Apparently, it's a group of women who get together regularly (in this case, no pun intended), to talk about any and everything while drinking different wines. Again, just because it's something I don't understand, doesn't mean it's not special to them. A very particular request came to my attention one day. They wanted custom wine glasses for their wine club. Zero hesitation. Within 72 hours a case of them had been created. Yes. I'm that good and that fast. I make shit happen. And I get shit done.

"Just because you don't think you can do something, is not the same as being capable."

What that means is simply this. If you have a deadline, need something created, or already have something and need to market the hell out of it, delegate. Find that person who wants to help you make more money. This is how you develop a strong team. The more solid, the more versatile, and the more driven your team is overall, the more you'll succeed. You're the coach, the scout, and the quarterback. What you say goes. Be solid and flex only when required (to benefit your business).

If you can do these few simple things, you will be more successful than you can possibly imagine. When I begin something, it's not to see if it will work, or how good it can go, no. I take what I do to the max.

"I wake up and I piss excellence every fucking morning."

So, with all these products and recognition, things are going great! I'll be honest, I didn't expect to get into retail and merchandising, but it was the natural flow of things. Weapons were my passion, my goal, and what I thought to be known for. Wrong! It was always marketing.

Chapter 17

Back to the weapon development side of things. Setting up weapons demos were amongst some of my all-time favorite things to do. Early on, the thought of hiring and then training professionals on how to use these weapons, and then having them do my military and law enforcement demos was the plan. I was in a suit and tie most of the week. I had no intention of going out to the middle of nowhere to shoot anything in a $2,500 suit. It just isn't happening. But then something changed. "These are your weapons. No one knows them better than you. No one knows how they are supposed to function better than you or exactly their intended purpose. You run the courses and show them exactly what they're missing that they desperately need." This caused me to think a lot. Not only is my tactical discipline better than most, due to non-stop training but I'd not seen very many people who can do what I can in these real-life situations. Not only was I going to now consider this, but there was one very big factor that I needed to consider. I'm no longer in the military. From personal experience, no one likes to be shown up by someone who is not currently enlisted. It almost looks bad. And can be considered somewhat of an embarrassment. So, my approach was crucial in this matter. I needed to display that I would always remain a Marine, just no longer on paper. I knew what they needed because I had been there. I wasn't some know it all off the streets without the knowledge and experience. I was giving back by paying attention to my country and the men and women who fought to protect it. I was showing support.

The fact that I did some weapons demos in a suit made me feel like a real asshole. Even to the point where someone very high up in the weapons industry compared me to Tony Stark. I can't say it didn't make me happy. The goal was to make some amazing military weapons and have them used by as many agencies on the planet as possible. And no matter what, it was going to happen. I was soon meeting with different Sheriff departments, other police departments, SWAT teams, as well as people who may or may not have worked for agencies and teams that exist or don't. Because when you market, you market to everyone. Even if they are not going to use your product, they are attached to an industry where someone they know will utilize your product. Now grossing over $100 million annually might sound like a lot. Because it is. But when you started with $45,000 cash, it's pretty insane.

If I can create a business in one of the most niche markets and within a few years be doing those kinds of numbers, imagine what I can do in a market that has way more clients. For the 9 years or so that I did was a celebrity bodyguard, a lot of those people were now coming back knowing the field I was in and suddenly wanted custom items. "Can you customize this kind of weapon as a gift, or do this one for me?" Before, most weapons were solid colors. Chrome, stainless, blued or black. Now people want Tiffany blue, hot pink this, purple and gold that. People wanted to bring me weapons they already had to have my people customized them based on my reputation. Reputation is everything. Most people who know me personally will be honest with you and say "Yeah, he's kind of a dick." But they will always follow up with something along the lines of "But he knows what he is doing and he is reliable." Those who are really close to me, the few there are, totally confide and trust me, and would often say things that even I don't believe. "He's passionate, he's caring and puts others before him." Those who say I am obnoxious I would be more likely to agree with.

"When you are marketing, the best thing possible is aesthetics. Visuals. Have something that makes people stop and go, "What the hell is that?""

My Truck had a massive 10" lift on it, oversized wheels and tires, and had my logo all over it. It could be seen from space! Or so it felt like it. It was a billboard. Everywhere I went, everyone knew my truck. I'd often get people messaging me in public through social media that they had just seen me. I would be going out to run errands and now I have a bunch of new clients. Then when I couldn't be anymore obnoxious, I took it one step further. Got new license plates on my oversized truck and muscle car. They read AR KNG. Why? Because my weapons system was primarily based upon the Armalite platform. And I was simply the best to both make and use them. So, why not show off? The more attentions, the more sales.

"ABM. Always Be Marketing."

Chapter 18

You grow your business to where you need a larger workspace, a larger building, even a larger warehouse. I was staying so busy at this point in my life that this was inevitably the next step. When you lease or rent a building, in a sense you are just giving your money away to someone else. So why not let that person be yourself? By owning your land, building or facility (if it's within reason and affordable), at the end of the day you are paying yourself. By building equity and structure to the land, you and your business increase in value. This can potentially cut down cost and expenses quite a bit. Plus, you own it. I soon began looking at places near tourist attractions. My initial thought was on a major freeway between Las Vegas, NV and the Grand Canyon. And this is why. The land is cheap. I can run my own power and water. Hundreds of thousands of people drive right by it all the time. And by allowing the public to come to the only place that has our products, I'd also allow them the opportunity to rent and shoot the weapons we were making for the government. No purchasing, just renting on our test range that would also be right on sight. How cool would that be? "You mean to tell me I can test fire guns that are not available to the public?" Exclusivity. Not only would we provide this, but the guests would also be able to see what projects we were working on for the future. To which would also include a massive gift shop of all our available merchandise. I spent a long time, scouting locations until I found the perfect spot. Just so happens, I found a place in the one spot people almost always stop at along this particular route. And it was perfect. If we were going to find a location for our business that ships products primarily, why not place it in a location where people will stop anyways. More sales. While I began to work out the logistics of this new location, even more awesome shit happened.

The Secret Service wanted a new weapon created. I got all the schematics they requested, the preferred caliber they'd like to use as well as any other potential customizations that might help. Military, Law Enforcement, celebrities, and now the Secret Service. Have you ever juggled chainsaws before? Good. Neither have I and that's exactly where I was at. A level of amazing that even shocked me. But one false move and everything could come crashing down. But that was not going to happen. Failure is not an option. Time to adapt and overcome. It seemed more often than most that I'd want to get input on an idea and right before that point would arrive, someone always asked me, "How are you going to get this done?" Somehow, I always get it done. Go with your gut, even when you are nervous. Playing it safe never got anyone anywhere. Don't believe me? Albert Einstein, Benjamin Franklin, Jackie Robinson, and even that amazing yet quite deranged lunatic whom I love so much, Elon Musk. Everyone at one point or another said these people were all bat shit nuts. Why? Because they didn't play it safe and thought in a way that others did not. Don't get me wrong, there's nothing wrong with playing it safe. However, this isn't about helping the elderly cross the road. This is about domination. And this story started with me in Federal Prison, not the bubble wrap factory. Taking chances, creating opportunities where one doesn't exist, and most importantly becoming the master marketer your company needs. Me helping you? Huge risk for myself. I'm stepping out of my normal everyday routine to help other businesses. My reputation is on the line for you. And that's a risk I am willing to take to help you and I succeed. Together we increase your revenue.

When it comes to taking chances believe it or not, there is some skill that goes into it. What can I gain? What can I lose? Should this go bad, what can I learn from it? By having my own facility with a test range is genius. Having one location where people can try our products. But how can I allow people all over the country experience the same thing if they are nowhere near me? RESEARCH! I decided to make a list of every single gun range and gun store with a range in the United States. This was not an easy task. But I did it. I was going to find a way to have my weapons (the top 3 most popular ones based on social media feedback), available to rent at as many gun ranges as possible. Within 36 hours, I had an attorney draw up all the paperwork necessary to get these deals done, and began emailing all the ranges on the list I had compiled. I explained that my company would cover any major maintenance on all firearms, extra parts and even provide the necessary training that the range instructors would need in order to show guests how to properly and safely handle these weapon systems. I would even cover the cost to all the ranges for all weapons included. Meaning, I'm giving these to you free of charge. My team fought me on this until they saw the bigger picture. Then they quickly agreed. I might spend $3,000-$5,000 for one range to carry our weapons, but that's a one-time expense. A marketing expense. A write off if you will. This was my advertisement in ranges across America. So, what was I doing? I was driving hundreds of thousands of customers both new and existing to spend more money at these ranges due to my new and exciting opportunity.

The ranges would advertise on their websites and social media the new weapons package that would become available for rent at their locations. Was this the big picture? Hell no!

When I spend money, it's to make money back. Of course, it's a marketing expense, but this was so much more than that. Not only did I cross promote the shit out of their locations with our product, but to rent this package, it would now cost you a minimum of $175 per person. I kept 60% and the ranges kept 40%. Of course, we ended up negotiating a variation of this percentage with different ranges in different states but it was always close to this number. I was streamlining a new source of revenue to their businesses that they did not have before. That's like free money for them. Now the $3,000-$5,000 that I had initially spent was the retail value of the weapons. My actual cost was no more than $1,250 in total to complete all of them for each location. Do you have any idea how many gun ranges there are in this country? Holy Santa Clause shit. There's a ton! It's a fairly substantial investment on my part with an even higher return.

Picture this. You own a business. Any kind of business, and I do nothing but bring you clients. You handle what you need to daily as clients just keep coming. Your online sales are increasing, your customer base is growing, and now everything you post is selling even quicker all because I am now bringing you customers from all over who want to purchase your product. How much is that worth to you?

If you work on music and you have a new single you are putting out on iTunes or whatever platform you sell it on, and we brought your fanbase up just an extra 100,000 more than it was at before, and you are also selling your songs for $.99 a piece, a $10,000 investment in yourself is suddenly an amazing idea for an entire year of marketing.

If your business is making $3,000 a day and I increase that for you, then $5,000 for a years' worth of marketing is an amazing idea for your business. Not only do you make your marketing dollars back in a matter of days, but you now have long term money coming due to an increase in your client and customer base. An extra six figures annually isn't so bad. Your income grows, which means you can spend more time doing the things you want to do that you didn't have time to do before. And I want to help!

My calculated risk to make a company gross over $100 million annually, worked. I did it. So can you. You know I actually flew to Seattle, D.C., and tons of other places because at first a few ranges didn't believe this offer. People are too used to the fact that no one gives anything away for free. Especially some next level military weaponry. This kind of thing in business just doesn't happen much anymore. I showed up, did my demo and left with everything that I'd brought with me, just to leave them wanting more. When I got home, I couldn't respond to emails fast enough. This is exactly what you want when conducting business. If people aren't bugging you, then market better.

And if you're not sure how, then pick up the phone and call me. I'll take it to the next level. I'll have so many people messaging you on social media and emailing you that you will have to hire employees just to handle that part of your business.

(You know what, now that this idea just formed, I'm going to give it to you! This was not planned and literally just popped into my head this very second. If your business has a product or service that I absolutely love, you'll give it to me, and not only will I drive hundreds of thousands in sales your way, but I will also market your product and service, personally, on my own social media pages at no extra charge. No extra fees. Normally I drive clientele to your business, but now I will take it even further. How about this, I show up at your business, have it filmed with my own crew and boost your sales even more! And you won't pay a single cent for any of this.)

Remember this. If I am successful, it means that you are also. It is a push and pull process. I push the clientele to you and you pull the money in. That's what I call teamwork.

Chapter 19

It began to seem like every time I opened my mouth it was for business. And that happened for a long time. People kept asking me, "Who designed this?" and, "Who designed that?" I designed everything myself. And more importantly, I knew where to place certain people in order for everything to work.

So where do I go from here? I make some time to find a great location. Start getting contractors together to see what it would cost for my new facility to get built and begin thriving. I was now set for the next major development in expansion.

When someone hears that you are expanding anything, they hear "more money". And now they want to figure out how they can become a part of that. It's not a bad thing. At this point to grow you may need some extra hands anyways. I mean, because now, you've got a lot on your plate and that is also a very good thing. Instead of taking my money and purchasing the land and construction of a new building and increasing product orders, there were now investors who wanted a piece of this action and take this business to a level even higher than where I was currently at. They all told me that with my marketing we could increase sales to well over $100 million annually. The part I heard was "well over". Although it's not an exact number, what it does tell me is that it's a number that continues to grow. And with your business, you should always look for ways that it can continue to grow.

At this point I needed a vacation. When you work incredibly hard, you play incredibly hard. However, when I go on vacation it doesn't always seem like vacation. People meet you, you meet them, they ask what you do for a living, and if they find what you do to be fascinating, the questions pile on in. And of course, you want to be polite as you never know who you just might meet.

When I go on vacation it's normally south of the border. Like really far south. To where everything is cheap, delicious, and no one gives two shits about who you really are. Unless you happen to own a Tequila company and somehow an exotic wildlife sanctuary. I'll admit, I love exotic animals and when I get around them, often times I turn into a big kid. An acquaintance of mine was always fascinated by what I did for work. But I was always fascinated by what he did. And when I am on vacation, I don't normally like to discuss business. I wanted to relax. He had the coolest monkeys, jaguars, cheetahs, and tigers at this sanctuary. So, I had a couple of drinks to calm my nerves and got the opportunity to play with some of these little guys. For you wildlife nuts, these animals have been rescued and live a much better life than most of us. This was a dream come true. I saw this snow-white tiger which at the time was only about 4 months old, with paws like a bear. Now if you've never had the opportunity to play with a tiger, I suggest you find the nearest one and immediately start wrestling with it. Side note; DO NOT DO THIS EVER. It was a joke and it can be insanely dangerous. I have to say that because someone will in fact read this then go and do it somehow, believing that's the key to success. It's not. I promise.

You become successful then find a safe happy baby tiger to play with. I promise you, your life will forever change. Taking little Tony home was an immediate though, although I couldn't. One his name wasn't really Tony and two, I was down there on a cruise ship. How could I possibly explain walking back onto the cruise ship. So, I spent an hour thinking about it and couldn't come up with anything good. Two things then happened. My buddy said he wanted to invest in my business and would give me the tiger as a down payment. Seriously? It reminded me of the Jack Benny skit where the homeless guy jumps out and yells at the passerby, "Your life, or your money!" and the guy pauses with no response. So, the homeless guy yells again, "Your life, or your money!" and the guy responds with, "Hold on. I'm thinking." Well, this is where I was at. Since I was a child, I have always wanted a tiger. For Hanukkah, I would often ask for one. I told my mom she could save on getting me eight presents and just spring for a tiger. Her response was often, "How about I spring my hand upside your head?"

So, I said that to say this. Sometimes in life, you may get offers you don't expect. Oftentimes, they can be amazing. Like the one with Tony. And it didn't end there. I had this country's government ready to invest and bring my brand to them. Somehow word got out that this country was interested in my weapons systems and half way around the world came yet another offer. And this happened all while on vacation. To be honest, vacation was all I really wanted. So, I'm driving through this country on vacation when through my social media, of all places, an official from one of the biggest Arab countries in the world was reaching out to me direct. This could mean cease everything weapons wise immediately and transfer everything, patents and all to this new country. Of course, the merchandise would still sell globally. But the weapons, designs, and everything else, would now be in a totally different country.

"Weighing your options can be tricky at times."

For instance, I'm a Jew, considering working with Arab countries, not for anything negative or illegal in any manner whatsoever but to make something bigger and better. We're now not just talking north of $100 million annually, but closer to $1 billion annually. By working in another country there are more clients worldwide that business can be done with. Without restrictions that the United States may have. Simple business move was how I viewed this. Ask Mark Zuckerberg. Yeah, we

61

use Facebook and it operates in the U.S., but headquarters is in a totally different country. Same with Google and several other major companies. Lots of companies are out of the U.S. and operate legally here within the states. Plus, in all honesty, $1 billion sounds way better than $100 million. I mentioned this option to a friend of mine and they thought it was great but might not be the safest option. Also, the U.S. might have some sort of competition issue now that I want to pull out and go somewhere else to expand. The country I would operate out of could now sell to a majority of the world. I could live virtually anywhere, I could do anything. Plus, I would now have the money to fund projects for even more beneficial weapon systems to both help and protect other nations. It's kind of like how Elon Musk went from making an electric car to a spaceship. Crazy, but he did it. That's a big fucking leap.

Now I was ready to consider the same option. But one thing seemed to be holding me back. I'm a Marine. I'm an American. And this is the country I once swore to protect. I had spent my entire career to this point fighting for this country. Protecting some of the most important and most influential people in this country. Although, I'm the child of an immigrant, this was now my country. I now had an indispensable amount of money at my fingertips and I was hesitating. Why now? I'm still going to make a buttload of money one way or the other. By doing it here in the U.S., I provide tons of jobs which helps hundreds of families, help put their children through school, even college and stimulate the economy with the amount of taxes my company would be paying. By doing it here, I would make an impact that could help generations to come. That truly felt great. Going to some country where I don't know anyone and helping people who don't know me and don't support me, that almost seemed like a slap in the face to everyone in this   country who helped me get to where I am now. I now needed a vacation from the one I was already on. When you are in a position to help the number one economy and country on the planet, that's a good thing. A handful of people get this opportunity and now the kid who once sold mistletoe for $1 a bag, was now there. Breaktime.

Chapter 20

Your business. Your product. Your service. Believe it or not, this is the big picture. You do make an impact to your community, even if that community is an online one. What you may see as something simple, someone else views as amazing. My suggestion would be this, give back. Keep doing what you are doing and don't stop. Be as successful as you possibly can. Bring others onto your team, your business, and expand with the focused thought that you are in fact making a difference. This is human marketing. Making people feel better about themselves, their lives, and their community. Marketing is everywhere. Marketing brings people together. If not for marketing, I guarantee you, I would have not met about 90% of the people I have worked with and know on a personal level.

"Marketing is more than sales. It's connecting. And when people connect it's like magic. Some people connect to become billionaires, some connect to make a new life, a child, who in turn will change the future for millions of people. To market is to connect, to connect is to bond, and a bond is for life."

If you don't have the answers to a problem at that exact moment just quit! I'm only kidding. Take a break. Go do something else. If you asked most who know me, "How much does he work?" Most would say non-stop. While it seems to be that way from perception, it's not truly this way by facts. I work out a lot. I have hobbies. Hell, I even have a son who is almost 21 years old and I am only 38. When I am stuck with a work issue or pretty much any issue at all that cannot be rectified immediately, it's then time to reset. Regroup. Your brain is a muscle and it gets tired when overworked. Just like in the gym. You can't workout 7 days a week without expecting fatigue to set in at some point. Your body will let you know that you need a break. You require rest to repair, grow, and reset. This way your strength is back at full for the next task. If you go into a project with half the energy or half the capabilities that you truly possess, you're going to get half ass results. By overworking your brain, you can actually do real harm to your business without even realizing it until it's too late. Go on a staycation with friends and family somewhere local or somewhere far if time permits.

If you are on a deadline with similar issues, I found something pretty cool that helps most people. Go visit your favorite business. But this time for an entirely different reason than you normally would go for. If you are a regular there, let them know. Tell them you have some questions and would like to speak to whoever is in charge. They would love to help you, trust me. By doing this, you would be surprised at the information you get. And from that, you may gain new ideas to help your own business overcome in an area that's lacking. Own a bar? Go visit some other bars during the week when it's slow and then on the weekend when they are slammed. See what they are doing to boost business if that's what you need to do. Go to a competing salon for hair services. See what they are or aren't doing. This will give you a lot of ideas without stressing yourself out. What products do they have, tools of the trade they are utilizing and the quality of what they do? I call this market research. Because this is the type of research that will change your client base. Potentially increasing it because clients now know exactly what you have and why they want to come to you versus the other places. Marketing!

So, I decided to keep things in the United States for my economy, my country, and fellow citizens so they could flourish. It seemed like the right thing to do. The irony someone pointed out to me wasn't lost. "You make weapons with the goal to make life better for people?" Yes. Yes, I do. Believe it or not, we will always be at war with someone. As sad as that is, it's the truth. Look at history and find a point in time when someone wasn't trying to take over or conquer. You won't. Even today we fight all types of wars. From protecting our country, to defending other countries who don't have the ability to defend themselves. Even to the local "War on Drugs". And war brings money for our country like you wouldn't believe. The money we make from war, trickles down into things sometimes as small as a business loan, car loan, and even stimulus checks. It's literally the most violent form of marketing aside from MMA and UFC fights that there is. These things go on to create Hollywood films, which also in turn produce hundreds of millions of dollars. For my particular business, I didn't stray and I maintained my true course, doing what I believed to be absolutely right, all for the right reasons. This is also known as sticking to the G-Code. I got back to designing the new facility, the location, how it would be set, as well as day to day operations.

Chapter 21

Having dinners with major investors, not intentionally to invest, just as friends to discuss what each other had been up to, can be quite fun at times. For instance, one time was a little crazier than expected. One of these guys was from Italy and one was from Israel. One owned a major portion of one of the biggest Cannabis distributors in Nevada, while the other owned a whole lot of strip clubs on the east coast. They had both been friends and competing with one another for years. They had both pre-ordered a brand-new rolls Royce that was set to come out on the market soon. Yet, they managed to get them before anyone else. And so, it went something like this. "Mine is better than yours." Here's the thing though, they were identical. If one got something, then the other had to get it as well as to not feel left out. However, the thing that got me was they both wanted to return them. Not because of quality or dislike, but because they both struggled with the USB port. Now I was laughing. What happened next made everything stop. Well, it was my reaction that caused everything to stop. The guy from Italy who must have been nearly 70, was with his girlfriend who was no older than 23 or 24. I guess her friend who was sitting right next to her told her what it was I did for a living. Before I knew what happened, my knee slammed into the bottom of the table interrupting everyone mid conversation. Her foot was rubbing my crotch. She was sitting right across from me at this long rectangular table with about 15 of us who were gathered for an evening to discuss fun and life. I did not expect anything like this. Suddenly the conversation turned my direction where I quickly apologized. The girl whose foot was slowly grinding my crotch was whispering to her boyfriend. I was nervous at first. But then he spoke and became fascinated by what I did for a living and wanted to know more. I was invited to this dinner by a mutual friend of ours who owns an exotic rental car agency. Want to rent a Lamborghini, Rolls Royce, or even a Bentley? He's your guy.

Suddenly a lot of interest was shown in the gun industry. Questions like profit margins, expected growth, sales, etc. You know basic business crap. They were very intrigued that I was the sole owner of it all. They were discussing investments and what kind of money they could throw around to put into the business. I just came for a few drinks, some good food, a beautiful view of the entire Las Vegas strip which was lit up and you could see for miles from this particular restaurant on this massive hill out east. Do you have any idea what it's like to answer all these questions while someone's rubbing on your junk? Nearly impossible. I thought I was about to explode. Trying to force the blood back to my brain so I didn't look like a bumbling idiot. She was loving this. And I know what you are thinking. And no, I did not sleep with her. I was there for business. Plus, you don't shit where you eat. That's why there's no restaurants called "The Bathroom."

This all happened on a Friday night. By Monday morning two offers of half million dollars each in cash, up front, for 5% of my business. And all I'd let happen for this offer, was to allow someone's girlfriend to fondle me under the table. That's when my wheels got turning. Not about the girl, although she was banging, but the investment opportunities. If I basically did nothing and two very successful people were tossing money at me, what would happen if I actually tried. What if I approached investor? I could easily get five to ten times as much. For money, you can go about it a number of ways. Venture Capitalists, Private Investors, Kickstarter, GoFundMe, and possibly even banks. In my case, banks were out of the question. And Kickstarter and GoFundMe weren't really intended for government contractors. I could have gone to a bank for the loan, however, a guy named J.P Morgan messed that up beyond all possibility. Back in the late 1800's this gentleman acquired a lot of defective weapons, and then flipped them to the U.S. Government in a massive scheme that could've injured many. And now because of this illegal deal that went down, Chase bank inadvertently will not loan money to anyone in the arms industry. Although my business plan was that of a fortune 500 company, no bank would touch it. Every single bank manager I met with was beyond impressed and regrettably had to inform us that no bank would ever work with us on a loan as long as we were in the arms industry. Well, that sucks. So, it's back to private investors.

You can't just ask people for money. They have it, and tons of people always ask them for it. Befriend some people, spend time with them, and go from there. Let them come to you. If done correctly, they will. People with money always want to make more. It's like basic logic. I found out I could not accept the money from the guys in the cannabis industry, because of the laws in the cannabis industry. Although what he did was legal on a state level, you cannot mix weed money with gun money. Guns are on a federal level and marijuana is still federally illegal. It's just something the government freaks out about. And the strip club guy, well he couldn't verify where most of his money was even coming from and a visit from the IRS was something I would rather avoid. Trust me, there's nothing more embarrassing than having your front door kicked in by an armed collections agency.

Imagine if you owed Verizon money for a cell phone bill, and you didn't realize it, so they showed up in a T.T. truck with automatic weapons and kicked in your front door! "Get on the fucking ground! Can you hear me now bitch!" You may laugh, and think it's even ridiculous, but the I.R.S has done this over less than what you owe on your cell phone bill. This, I didn't want. No one wants that. But it happens. I abided by every law getting into the gun industry. Even little shit. I didn't screw around at all. Three things you don't ever play with; guns, the government, and their money. It might be your money to temporarily hold onto, but we all know who it really belongs to. Okay, maybe guns you can play with if you are trained well enough like me. But the other shit, don't even think about it.

Let's say you are in a similar position and would like to approach an investor, but not quite sure how to do so. The one thing people love, are gifts. It makes them feel special, sometimes even important. I don't care who you are. Young, old, rich, or even broke, everyone loves to receive a gift. And what happens when you receive an unexpected gift? We all want to know immediately, where did it come from, and who is it from. If your business makes a specific product, give it away to potential investors. This will pique their curiosity and soon they will be approaching you. Even if it's not something from your business and you would like to make an introduction, often times a nice bottle of good scotch will do. You have to spend some to make some. This is one of the best lessons in marketing.

And if a bottle of something expensive isn't for the person you would like to approach, then find something unique. Something not a lot of people may have. Possibly something that they will show off to their close friends and colleagues. And of course, some of this takes research. Learn about the person you would like to approach. The worst thing you can do is gift something to someone that may offend your potential contact. They will remember you and do everything to possibly avoid you from here on out as well as tell all of their friends. Know your audience.

Chapter 22

Where are your marketing dollars going and how are they being utilized? You would be surprised about the gun industry. Just because someone doesn't own a gun, doesn't mean they aren't fascinated by them and what they stand for. Weapons represent power. Movies are filled with guns. Many actors don't own a single firearm, yet they use them in every single movie they make. And yet, one of your favorite actors who has "a very particular set of skills" is anti-gun in real life, and 90% of his films he is seen carrying or using one. Doesn't matter how many times someone is taken, he's always armed.

So, what did I do? I did a lot of research. Got some inside information and found some items that were incredibly rare. What I was approaching investors with was something they'd never expect in a million years. When you give someone, a gift valued at $30,000-$40,000 each, you are definitely going to get some attention. Some were even speechless. The look on someone's face when they opened this is something I had personally never seen before. Only once, when I bought my son an NBA championship ring from his favorite team for Hanukkah one year. But not for a complete stranger. I had left many stunned. Now that's how you capture someone's undivided attention. Throw them off. Do something so unexpected that even people in your industry have to say, "What the fuck?!" I never do just one thing at a time. So, while I was doing my research to find this perfect gift, I was now chatting with the company that recently trained actor and legend Keanu Reeves from the John Wick film series. Ever seen that guy shoot in real life? You

70

should. It's some of the most impressive real life shooting I have ever seen any actor do in my life. Usually, it's all bullshit and video effects. But not this time. Keanu was killing it on the range. Johnny Utah is the real deal, ladies and gentlemen. I was discussing getting my weapons onto a few television shows and into some movies as this company specializes in that sort of thing. I do a lot when it comes to marketing. And I will stop at nothing to get my product out there.

So, my gift research went a little something like this. I looked into the gun market. On the side most don't get to see. Looking into what companies were doing deals with whom and what, if anything, was about to change drastically. And I found it after two days of searching. The military had just signed a deal with a major arms company. A Belgian brand if you will. Very well made and used by many of our current military members. So, the market was about to be completely bare when it came to a certain line of something they specifically made. They make one of the most important weapons that we use in combat for fire suppression. A belt fed automatic M249-SAW. Real quick, just google it and see what it is so you have an idea of what this is all about. Look up a video on YouTube as well so you can see how it functions. Did you wet yourself yet? Because I did. Only a handful of people on the planet will ever get to shoot one, and those are primarily active military members. Civilians, not so much. There may be a couple of cities in the entire United States that have a range where you may rent one and fire off a few rounds. This is not some custom handgun or rifle. This is what I like to call a game changer. Now, what exactly was my plan? This. My plan was to buy the last handful of M249-SAWs available on the market and ensure they were converted for civilian use, (meaning they were set to semi auto). They were still identical to the military standard issue versions in every single way, except for now they were completely legal for civilians to own. The problem was that supply was limited. I locked the last truckload that were available in the entire country and had them shipped from all over immediately. A few things were frowned upon but I muscled my way into buying every last one available on the market at once. This was nearly a $1.5 million dollar purchase by the time everything was said and done. And this was also happening right in the middle of relocating the business to the middle of the desert and building an entirely new facility from the ground up. I didn't exactly advertise what I was doing as I wanted to surprise each investor. Can you imagine getting a gift like this? My guess is they would have mounted it in their office on the wall or had a home office that proudly displayed this rare symbol of immaculate power. And you're probably wondering to yourself, why on earth would I give someone a gift that would cost nearly $30,000? Because of the actual value. Not the retail. But what it actually was valued to the individual themself. This is an opportunity to discuss business. To build a friendship. Not asking for a handout, but now a friend who wanted to help another friend make money for both of us. Now it's a win-win situation. When you invest in a friend who is valuable and has a keen understanding of making money, you both will be on the same page very soon.

"By giving an investor a gift on this level, you can easily leverage an interest in any business you present."

We are not talking about a little $100,000 investment. I just gave you a $30,000 gift that only a handful of other people in the entire country have. We are talking a potential of him or her investing a minimum of $500,000 - $1,000,000 into my business. Now multiply that by how many people I have given this gift to. That kind of potential can change the course of many people's lives for several years to come. When you pull up and hop out with a case that you are now dragging around on wheels, and you explain that you have a gift for someone, heads turn and eyes focus. At first, it's almost like doing a sales pitch. Let's put it this way. One investor I had met with, whom I gifted this vey awesome piece of machinery to asked me almost immediately, "What is it you want from me?" I responded, "No strings attached. But I would like to borrow your Lamborghini Aventador for the weekend and for you to consider investing a small amount in my weapons company." I left him with a copy of the updated business plan, a portfolio of three-year projections, and walked out of his office with an insane amount of confidence. Climbing into that Lamborghini Avanzado with the biggest shit eating grin you can imagine made me not even want to return for my muscle car. And I didn't. I had someone else go and pick it up.

"When you think outside the box, opportunities are endless. You are only limited by your imagination."

I walked in with a gift, and left with a $400,000 car. That weekend was by far one of the most enjoyable business weekends I'd ever had. While the Aventador was in my possession, I attended several more business meetings and was sure to be seen pulling up. Between the car and the gifts, what was left to be said? If you look successful, you will be successful. Now, when you are involved in certain industries it is in your best interest to keep certain types of friends. In my industry, the weapons industry, those were politicians. I can't stand politics. Although I am a Marine, I do not vote. It's one thing to fight and protect the citizens of this great country, but it's another to be involved in politics. Not my thing. But if you are involved with weapons on this level, this is a must. I didn't attend political fundraisers or anything that I should have. Well, I did attend one. For an attorney who was running for Judge. At the time, I thought she was great. I had no idea that in the near future she would be the center of many lawsuits and the reason so many people across this country lost their homes during one of the toughest times this nation has ever faced. Man, this chick was clueless. I was beginning to think she got her law degree from Craigslist. She didn't know very much about the law and she was also the primary reason I ended up in prison longer than I was sentenced for.

Chapter 23

Business meetings were going well. During this time, I was considering a lateral move. I spoke to a few people about completely selling my weapons company just to see what offers would come in. Should've taken it at the time. I probably would have my own island by now. But you would never get to read this book. So, a few months later, plans are drawn up for the new building and facility site. At this point, so much was happening. Everything was going well. I didn't have an assistant, as I enjoyed being hands on and involved in as many calls and meetings as possible. Which I didn't need to be in, but hey, I enjoyed learning new things that pertained to my business. When your business is taking off, these are things you want to be involved in. Get an assistant to help you schedule appointments and take calls that you don't necessarily have to be on. I ended up getting someone who would attend meetings for me, but would always say at the end of the meetings, "We can't make any decisions at this moment until I get final approval from him." They know who him was. And until I reviewed everything that I was involved in, I never moved forward without a second and sometimes even a third review.

I began to have all these random social media models pop up out of nowhere. They suddenly wanted to do photo shoots with our products. I didn't have to be there for any of that. With millions of followers, my brand was being posted somewhere daily for millions to see. I would gradually update the public via social media about our growth, expansion projects, and the new test range that would be open to the public.

Although all of this was going well, I wasn't quite ready to sit back. I had to look through contracts almost nightly. I was always up late on the government websites, logged in, and scanning through hundreds of contracts every single night. I always kept busy. The goal of this business was to get to a point where I could spend more time with family, but I didn't see it coming fast enough. Many nights I would come home and my son was already asleep. By the time I had awoken, he would already be gone for school. I lived with my son, just him and I. And often times in one week I would be lucky to see him on a Sunday afternoon. I would do my best to come home early enough as much as possible to at least ask my son how his day was or to have a super late dinner and conversate with him. I wanted to give him a great life and not be limited by certain things due to the poverty I endured. I was destined to succeed.

Every so often there would be a free Friday or Saturday night. We would rent movies, play video games, and talk about whatever he wanted. Every time I would check my phone there would be some message related to work. Some of my favorite messages had absolutely nothing to do with my business at all.

Due to the amazing growth on social media that my brand displayed, I began to get some very interesting requests. People would ask if they could pay me to post their business on my page for 24-48 hours at a time. When I saw people were offering me up to $1,500 per day to post some of their items, I didn't think it would be a bad idea. I post your business in my feed, you get a quick 20,000 views, maybe even a bunch of new customers. They made their money back sometimes within a few hours and I managed to get some serious cross marketing going on. This was stuff that was coming in nightly just on the side. From all over the world. At this time though, I was more focused on my own business, occasionally helping people here and there. One day I went to a local falafel restaurant that a friend of mine had opened. He had been there for about a year. Just for fun, I posted a quick video about his place. He called me that evening to tell me he had more sales that single day due to my posting than any day since he opened.

Now that everything was in order, it was time for one last push. A home developer I knew was interested in throwing some serious money my way. This was the down payment for the land I was about to purchase for the new facility. Everything was going to change forever. I mean, how close was I to owning my own company jet, a fleet of vehicles, and ramping up my employee roster. It's like that rush of excitement when something so good happens that you are not even sure how to react. And that's exactly what happened. It was like this sudden blur and everything seemed to happen in the blink of an eye.

Now before I proceed, let me make something very clear. We are all human beings. We have all made mistakes in life. Everything from the famous leaving your cup of coffee on the roof of your car and not realizing it until you suddenly hit the brakes, just to have coffee spill all over your car, to picking up the kids late from school, spacing on a meeting, or forgetting to make a payment on a bill. Mistakes are all relative and we all make them. We can all tell if they are malicious or not. Was it intentional, careless or truly something that could have and would have happened to a thousand different people had they been in the same position? What about a mistake that involves you, but you had no idea it happened? No way of knowing anything could possibly have happened. Now if someone kills someone that would be a pretty fatal mistake, but we are talking about something simple that could happen to the average person on any given day. Should someone have to pay for every single mistake they have ever made in their life? And should someone have to pay for someone else's mistake? If someone volunteers to pay for someone else's mistake that's altogether a different story. By all means, pay for the coffee and shorts that were ruined due to a misstep in someone's day. But this isn't that.

My life hit a brick wall harder than a crash test dummy. Imagine waking up in the passenger seat of a car as it's going off the edge of a cliff. What would you do? What could you do? Nothing. Not a mother fucking thing. And that's exactly what happened. My life was on cruise control in a car that could comfortably do 150 miles per hour with no brakes, approaching a dead end without warning.

In the world of big business, many are not aware that some larger companies have goals to shut down the competition one way or another. I never really saw myself as anyone's competition besides myself. I tried to outdo myself every single day. And in most industries, that's perfectly acceptable. In mine, not so much. In all honesty, I was the new guy on the block. Other contractors wanted to know exactly who I was and how I had established so quickly and so successfully all by myself. Well, those are my secrets to success. And I don't just give those away for free. This did not sit well with some people. But I never let the negativity bother me or bring my spirits down. And neither should you. I could have thrown my hands up and accepted defeat. But that's not what happened.

Chapter 24

September 6th, 2019. Friday morning at 7:30 A.M. I was getting ready to throw on my suit jacket and walk out the door to work. What I saw through the windows, almost all the way around my entire home, looked like the invasion of Fallujah. My home was being surrounded by more federal agents than I could count. I saw people running everywhere to surround the entire property. I could clearly see silhouettes of everyone with rifles and handguns. The only thing going through my head was, "What the fuck is happening?" I couldn't even guess. That's when I breathed a sigh of relief and said, "Maybe they're at the wrong house. This happens a lot and they make more mistakes than most." They weren't here for me. So, I opened the door to what seemed like an additional 40 more Federal Agents in cargo shorts and the typical "undercover" outfits pointing their weapons right at my face. Holy shit! And again, I was a little uneasy, but unfazed because I was pretty sure they were at the wrong house. Just a simple miscommunication like always. You know how when you see a SWAT tank accidentally tear into the wrong home, it was just like that. As soon as I stepped out of my home, the first agent asked if I was home alone. I explained that I was and I believe they have the wrong house. He immediately said my name and followed up with, "We've got the right house." I looked around, and the few neighbors I had due to the location I lived in were out and filming this event. So, I decided to play on it. "All this for me?" I responded with a shit eating grin? The "Special" Agent in charge said, "Yeah. And more are on the way." You've got to be shitting me.

I knew I was good. But nobody is that good. I had never really been in trouble my entire life, and now, what seemed to be every Federal Agent in the western hemisphere, were on my front lawn. This, my friend, is how you know you have mastered marketing! Mind you, I work hard and don't cut corners with anything that I do. Want to know why they were there? Well so did I. But I wasn't about to find out anytime soon.

I waited for what seemed to be hours. But Ashton Kutcher never showed up. I went straight to court. Then straight to prison. No phone calls. No questions. No nothing. Easily one of the most uneasy moments of my life. The prosecutor said I was a flight risk and a danger to the community. Wait until you hear what I was charged with. Filing a false document. Now hear this. Not only did this document not exist, but everyone seemed to be lost through this entire case. The prosecutor, the judge, my attorney and even all the Feds that kept showing up to court. No one could answer any questions as to what happened like any other case. It started to get weird as in almost unbelievable. I was in the wrong place. This was for certain. So, I sat in prison for over a month with no contact or communication. Then suddenly I was brought back to court. I was thinking this got figured out and these bogus charges would be dropped. I believed I was about to be released due to some mistake, yet again, that they made. And what do you know, I was wrong yet again! They are not allowed to admit mistakes, so taking shit to the next level is their way of correcting their own errors. No one wants to be embarrassed so they get angry, and their way of getting angry was this.

I was dragged into court, shackles, black box and all. Surrounded by Federal Marshalls on all sides. I was told these charges were not being dropped but in fact I was being superseded with a new indictment. Now not only did I allegedly fill out some document incorrectly that magically no one could locate, but now I was being charged with even crazier shit. What happened next cannot even be explained. There's no possible way to convey this sort of feeling. The most difficult part of what came next was keeping from snapping right out of those cuffs and defending myself. When you're cornered and there's no way to explain yourself...what do you do? What can you do? And so, this is what happened.

I was being charged with several counts of "International Arms Dealing" and "International Arms Trafficking" for a total of 60 years in Federal Prison. My brain was unable to even form a thought at this juncture. Not only was this untrue, but now I was 1000% sure they had the wrong person. But how could they be this wrong? I mean the cops shoot the wrong people all the time, people go to jail and prison for being in the wrong place at the wrong time, we know the government messes up more than you can imagine. But on this level? This is like Lord of War level. They said I was way too calm while going through this process. Well, no shit! I was trying to process the craziest shit I had ever heard in my entire life. What was I supposed to do? Freak out like a lunatic?

At the end of the day, I'm a businessman. I know how to handle every situation that I am somehow involved in. It's one thing to mess up and put yourself in a position like this, but entirely another for someone else to do something of this magnitude and you end up in this predicament.

Now, as bad as all this sounds, it's not what you think. When they said I was facing 60 years in prison I couldn't stop laughing. They explained that this was a serious matter. I guess they thought I was crazy for laughing. I think anyone might freak out a little bit if they just heard they were facing 60 years in Federal Prison. But not me. I immediately knew it was a joke. Don't get me wrong, these were very real charges, and this was a very real court room. And I had been spending way too much time in a very real prison. It took nearly a year before I managed to figure everything out. They said two things that told me I was even better at marketing than expected. "Allegedly", they found over 5,000 of my company's weapons just south of the border in the hands of some of the biggest cartels ever. And then they "found" over 20,000 more in Croatia. This went on and on. They found over 100,000+ weapons that "allegedly" belonged to me, all around the world in countries that we were not supposed to be doing business with. Now due to legalities, and several, several threats from the government as well as my own legal counsel, I am not allowed to disclose any more information than that. I was told specifically that I could disappear for good if any of my case gets out to the public as to why it's sealed. So, what more can I say about it this? DAMN!

Talk about marketing. Now again, this still isn't the end. In fact, you're probably wondering how can this possibly get any better at this point. Well, I'm here to tell you it gets much better. In fact, it gets so good. Quite possibly about 11 hours later, upon leaving the courtroom and returning back to my cell, 2 hours away, in the middle of fucking nowhere, I get amazing news. The "International Arms Dealing" and "International Arms Trafficking" charges were dropped without question. Oh yeah, it gets so much weirder. The ATF disappeared off this case like a damn magic show. The prosecutor, who I found out later was a woman, but looked identical to McCauly Caulkin, wanted to nail my ass more than anything in the world. She said she wouldn't stop until I got the max time. She disappeared also. A prosecutor who worked for over 20 years in this field… suddenly drops the case? Gives it to a brand-new prosecutor? I was his first case. What the hell was going on? Everything I had was seized by the government and there was no chance of getting anything back.

I'd like to call this a learning experience. Not just for myself, but for many on both sides of this. Suddenly everything vanished. Something very big happened. Bigger than you will ever know or be able to legally find out about. They said the only way I would be allowed to get out of prison was to plead guilty to a minor "document" charge, and accept a twenty-four-month sentence. I refused. So, they said I would never be let out of prison ever until I accepted this deal. Here was the catch. I had to agree to get out of the gun industry for good and never ever try and make new weapons patents or designs ever again. But I would be free after 24 months to do anything else I wanted except for designing and creating weapons for the government ever again. It wasn't a bad deal when you thought about how powerful the government is and what they are capable of.

So, what did I do for 24 months in Federal Prison? MORE MARKETING!!

Chapter 25

The first thing people do when they get to prison is ask for your paperwork, to see if you are a snitch, a chomo, or a cop. If this is so, you get one chance to get transferred otherwise you won't live to see another day. I'm clearly none of that weird shit. But I used this opportunity to market myself. When someone asked for my paperwork. I said no. I told them to go get a phone and look me up and who I was. And that's exactly what happened. Within a few days everyone knew I was a big deal in the gun industry. But that's not what my goal was. I started to get all kinds of business questions. How to invest money, where to invest, how to market their already existing businesses, and so forth. I started to get so many questions that I decided to meet with the Warden and see about teaching a business class. This way inmates could also get time off their sentence for programming. I was beyond surprised when the Warden agreed. The Warden knew I was a Marine like him as well. He told me to let him know what I needed for the class and that we can make it happen immediately. Going from creating and operating a business that could generate over $100 million a year to teaching a room full of the biggest convicts you've never heard of. And they all wanted to learn something legit. So, I gave them what I knew. I taught them how to complete business plans, how to budget, market, and everything else that went into creating a business from the ground up. Although I was very explicit with, "Do not tell me where your money is coming from.", it was still fun and we spoke with a lot of hypothetical situations. We discussed nothing illegal and for many, it felt like a first. Between classes, I was being paid in commissary, often a new watch, shoes, food, mp3 players, and more to help put together business plans specifically for them. One on one time, people were willing to compensate me for. Before long, people were showing me businesses they had on the outside as well as their social media accounts. Yes, even in prison, where there's a will, there's a way. They asked if I could redo their pages and to show them some simple marketing tips and tools in order to increase views, client base, and revenue. I did a lot of this oftentimes right from the comfort of my own cell. Business never stops, no matter where I go. People always have questions and that's good. I'm here to help.

For myself, being at the first prison I was at, I had access to a computer and a flash drive. Altogether just for fun, I knocked out 6 complete business plans with the potential to earn in the billions with the right team. I didn't just sit in prison and let time fly by. Doing something every available minute was the goal.

I had several people asking me to help them with marketing. It got to a point where the people on the phone that I had spoken with had friends who owned businesses that also needed help as soon as I was released.

Whether it's the fact that I had worked with people like Jennifer Lopez, Lady Gaga, 50 Cent, or any other high-profile individual like that, or that I simply just knew what the fuck I was doing, they wanted my help. Someone even suggested that I do it full time. I had never really considered this. Had I done marketing regularly, for every business I had, and primarily throughout my entire life? Yes. This made perfect sense. This, I was great at. This is what I had mastered. And not once, did I ever think marketing is the business that I should be in. If I'm that damn good at making money, then I can make quite a few other businesses even more. I spent an entire week developing my business plan for AEY MARKETING. A Global Social Media Marketing Company. And when I say I spent one solid week doing this, I don't mean like you, at home, 20 minutes a day for 4 days. I spent 7 days, entire days, aside from scheduled prison movements, I'm talking damn near 19 hours a day working on this business plan. While I was working out, I made notes. While I was in bed, I made notes. I had a pen and notepad with me on every part of the prison that I was at.

Now what is AEY MARKETING? It's exactly what it sounds like. It's a formulated way, to guarantee a client increase to anyone's business, anywhere in the world at any time. Doesn't matter where you live. If your business has any type of websites, or social media, I GUARANTEE you an increase in business anywhere from 25%-125%. We're talking a revenue increase. I'm saying you focus on your business and all the things that need to be done, and I'll focus on bringing that increased client base to you. With my formula, you will see your client base grow before your very eyes. You will see actual numbers of clients, and not wonder how many people are supporting your business or making purchases.

You'll now have definitive proof. You'll see where your support is coming from. What cities, what countries, and the best times of the week to begin posting new items and sales to attract the majority of your demographic. The best thing about my marketing, is you get a trending list of information daily. You get to see what age groups are more interested in your products before each quarter so you can stay ahead of the curve. By doing this, you know where to begin marketing your products, in which fields and who your target audience is. It's one thing to guess the age group and type of people who may or may not be interested in your products or service, but it's even better to know ahead of time how to increase your sales. Let's not leave out a mass group of people who want to spend their hard-earned money on your company. It's almost like having insider information to your own business. The more you know about your business, the more successful you will be.

It's like this also. You have a product or service and you're not quite sure the age group that it may be most appropriate for, as some things are catered for specific ages. It could be for teens, young adults, college students, married people, and even senior citizens. Businesses are paying millions every year to do this sort of extensive research and this eats up a lot of time. I do that for you as you go. This way it saves you the time and the money that your business needs.

"When I realized the only competitor I have is myself, I knew that I could help millions of people worldwide."

This time I'm not in a niche market that some people dislike or might have an issue with. Now this is something that literally everyone needs on a level playing field. Now you have an amazing solution to a problem that everyone with every business has. Marketing. No need to waste money on television ads, radio ads, or billboard ads. Do that later when you have the money already coming in. For now, the best thing you can do is make money and increase your client base. This way money is coming in before it goes out. So, I pitched my service to several people over the phone, by email, and had it passed along to see what other businesses thought, and it looks like I have found my new groove. Logo, website, social media, all created from the comforts of my very own prison cell. How about that? A lot of people tell me that I am very resourceful and I always tell them, "You don't know what you are actually capable of until you're locked in a prison cell." Just like you Mr. and Ms. Business owner. When you get stuck, and want the world to know about your product or service, your job then becomes to delegate. Reach out to someone who can make your life much easier by providing the relief you need.

Chapter 26

People ask me all the time, "How do you do it?" "How do I do what?" How do I get someone's social media page to 50K, 1 million or even 5 million legitimate followers? The answer is easy. The work however is not. It took me several years of research, study, and to befriend some people who work for places such as Google to learn the things I needed to help my own business develop. I put together a fool proof formulated plan that is guaranteed to increase your revenue by up to $100,000,000 annually. My company locates clients and customers who are already interested in your products and services. Not by paid advertising.

When people are on social media scrolling through their feed and they see a sponsored advertisement, most of the time they do what I do and skip right through it. No one likes commercials anywhere. On the radio, we change the station. For TV, we now have DVRs and other ways to watch without being interrupted. However, when someone is interested in what you have, they immediately follow your page and become a fan of your service, your product, and is now a potential client or customer. So, what I do is track down the people who are already interested in what you have. I cross market your fanbase to all platforms that are relevant. Trust your bank account. It is better to have people who want to follow and support your business rather than paying for an advertisement that you hope someone will not only see, but now also click on and then navigate when they finally get to your page. Someone who isn't familiar with what you have most likely will not stick around and go through your page. I go right to the source. To your customer. To your client. Right to their pocket. Listen, I'm not saying don't advertise, what I am saying is make more money. If you have the money to blow on advertisements, do it. If it won't break the bank have fun with it. But if you want to advertise your company on a pro MMA or UFC fighters' apparel on a televised event, well, then I can give you direct access to that far cheaper than anyone else can possibly even consider. What I won't do is waste your time or your money. I was in your shoes so I know exactly how it is.

When I was younger, it was difficult for me to figure out exactly who my demographic was. I had no way to know exactly who was interested in my products. So, asking everyone was my only option at that time. Of course, things were much different before the internet really took off, but there was still a formula guaranteed to work. There was a method to madness if you will. It would almost seem as if I was asking every person I saw if they were interested, and in the beginning that's exactly what I did. You don't know who will say no, until you ask. But do you just take that no for an answer? Absolutely not. It was rare that I could not close a deal and in those rare occasions I always asked, "If you were to be interested, what would it take for that to happen?" See what I am doing now? Gathering information and feedback from potential buyers to turn those same exact people into actual buyers. Market research. Keyword, market. You could just walk away but then you lose valuable information to help potentially structure and progress your business.

With this calculated formula on retrieving clients, I couldn't lose. Soon customers who never would have been, were buying items they didn't even need. Did they want them? Sure. Because it made them feel good. I made it feel as though this was something they absolutely wanted more than anything at the moment. They didn't have to. They want to.

"Create the want, create the connection."

Think about this. What exactly do you want out of your business? To grow? To be memorable? Find the meaning of why you are doing what it is you are wanting to do or are already doing and then you will be on the path to success. It's okay to be rich and prosperous. What's not okay is to beat your head against the wall repeatedly by doing the same thing over and over and expecting different results. That's just insanity. And there is a huge difference between not giving up and being absolutely crazy. It may be uncomfortable at first to do something that you are not used to, but I can say we all feel that way when embarking on a new journey. A new path. You have been doing what you know for so long that it's now muscle memory. Time to shake things up a bit.

Making money is uncomfortable. Making a lot of it is downright scary because it's new. But soon you will enjoy it. I guarantee it. And soon, that will be your new normal. If you are already working hard, let's fine tune a few minor things to change the outcome drastically in your favor. Again, buying a new home, or a car that you have always dreamed of can be often intimidating, but I can assure you it's well worth it if you believe so. The nicer the stuff is that you have, clearly the more successful you are. Let your hard work pay off. Remember the words, will and determination? You will make your dreams come true because you are determined to do so. As long as you don't give up and you project success, you will be successful.

Ask for help. Maybe you are like me and asking for help really isn't your style. Well guess what? It needs to be if you are a business owner. When I market, I am asking the public for help. When I market your product or service, we are asking the public yet again for help. "Please help me" or "Try my product" is saying, "I need your help". The best kind of marketing brings in the best kind of help there is. People who are going to give you, their money. Marketing is a strategic and very fashionable way to publicly ask for help from every person you don't know. If your business is a service, then you're practically begging for people to not only buy from you, but you are also asking them to now trust you. "You want me to trust you and I don't even know you?" Most people have trouble inviting a total stranger into their home nowadays, but every day without thinking about it, we allow strangers to place their hands all over our body for services such as a massage. Yet without thinking about it again, a lot of those same people would not be seen in public in a bathing suit. Proper marketing brings trust. With trust, your options are limitless. If you market something the wrong way, it can scare customers off and make them avoid you, like in-laws. It all comes down to your business introduction.

Chapter 27

Although I do not engage in the branding side of marketing much, I will touch on it briefly as I have in fact excelled in this area. First of all, what is branding? Identity. Everything from your logo, shape, design, colors, and products. Staying warm and engaging is always key and very crucial. Choose colors appropriate to your industry. Not sure what they are? Good. Because it doesn't actually matter. Of course, you can look at what others are doing and quite possibly after a while it will start to blur together making it difficult to tell them apart. Now that's not a good thing. You want your business to stand out. And there isn't necessarily a right or wrong way to do this. It's all in your approach. The more creative the better. You want your customers to see something eye catching and possibly make them smile. Remember, I created one of the fastest growing weapon defense companies in the nation and my feedback, was that people kept saying our logo resembled something as a Marvel logo. Someone even said it reminded them of a company owned by the character Tony Stark. Some people even put their logos on t-shirts just to give them away. Cell phone battery chargers, pens, stress balls. You can put your company logo on literally anything. If it is something that someone will use on a daily basis, then do it. When it comes to marketing, knowing where to put your marketing dollars is the key,

Take what happened to Paul Rudd's character in the movie "I Love You Man". His friend posted funny pictures of him all throughout the city of Los Angeles on massive billboards showing him as the fun realtor that he in fact is. Could this be something smart to do in the real world? Absolutely! The market you are attracting and the returns from that marketing investment in yourself will pay for itself for years to come. Now would you do the same thing if you owned a business who sold things strictly online? No way. These are all things I have taught in classes. Never limit yourself.

Business structures change slightly, but marketing itself does not. People to this very day still go door to door. I used to have to wait to get my favorite thin mint cookies every year. But even the Girl Scouts have changed the way they do business. They stepped up their marketing efficiently if I might add. Not only is there an app now that tells you where these magical cookies are being sold at, but they are now even selling in more strategic places. Normally you would find them at grocery stores, strip malls, and other places like that, however, now they have begun to get out in front of dispensaries. Because who loves cookies more than someone who is about to go home and get baked! These kids are definitely thinking outside the box.

Let's take marketing down to its rawest form. Just people. No billboards, no social media, no gimmicks. Just people. I know more than most when it comes to marketing in various areas. But to know people is an entirely different story. For example, in prison, marketing is huge. You are probably shaking your head in confusion, so I will break it down. In prison the people who watch you more than anything are other inmates. They study each other like it's the fucking National Geographic channel. Why? Because this is how you stay alive for one. You learn what's about to happen, learn who it's going to happen to, and exactly when it will happen. These are what we call trends. And here there are no notes, no advertisements, just good old inside information. Probably why Martha Stewart did so well. The other side of this is how to know what group of people you are going to hang out with. This can also lead to a life and death situation. Roll in the car as they say in prison, and even your own people can kill you. For those of you who have never been to prison, allow me to break it down in a comparable way.

Prison is just like college. It just happens to be the part of college where you join a fraternity. How do you know which is for you? (Granted your parents haven't been in one which they ultimately just want you to be a part of). You go from table to table and check out what they offer. See if their goals and politics are in line with your own. What can you achieve in life by picking one fraternity over another? It all comes down to networking. You can pick one to be a part of while still having friends in another. These are the people who support you and you support them indefinitely. A lot of politicians come from similar fraternities that remain in contact for life. Some even wear rings and have symbols that one another may only recognize. Again, another form of marketing. In prison however, the differences usually default to race, tattoos, and/or religious beliefs. Although there are no written rules, nearly every single person on the inside abides by them, and that means every race. Myself. Because I am middle eastern and Jewish on top of that, primarily you are defaulted to run with the whites. However, in my situation, being a Jew, this does not work in prison. Swastikas are a "You're not welcome" insignia for my people. This is also a form of marketing at the most primal level. And just because one race or one culture does not sit and eat or spend time with another race, due to prison politics, does not mean they cannot do business with one another. Competitors, believe it or not, at some point will do business with one another if it's mutually beneficial. During these deals, personal feelings are set aside as money is above everything else. Even in a life and death situation.

People operate on an instinctual level. We know what other people want and need. We possess intuition, knowledge, and feelings to know exactly what can be done in most situations. Tapping into that is the key. We all have this capability. However, with so many distractions in life, sometimes we are too busy to see certain things that can help us, therefore can be detrimental to our business, which is our livelihood. Just like in prison. I've learned about people on many different levels. Even more so than before I went to prison. I have worked with the most successful people, college educated people, to the biggest gang members and drug dealers this globe has ever seen. Ironically, it's safe to say, I know people.

Chapter 28

"You will adapt. You will overcome. And you will succeed at what you do."

Paying attention is what I like to call reverse-marketing. Like counter surveillance, you are watching, to see who is watching you. You definitely need someone like this working for or with your business. Definitely don't go to prison and do the extensive research that I have done. Does it help? Absolutely! But please try and avoid this at all costs. It's not necessary. The fact of the matter is, extensive research is key to all you do. If you don't do it, make sure you get someone who does. You're in charge, you make the decisions, and making the decision to be successful should be a daily priority for you and your business. Watching over your shoulder as to not to get stabbed while eating, is not the kind of research you need. But it does teach you a lot about people.

In order to trust others, you must first begin to trust yourself. I can't tell you how many people I have spoken with who asked me about marketing and did not immediately take my advice. I wasn't offended. However, they all came back months later and said they had tried things a different way and didn't get the results they were looking for. And finally asked me to sign on and help them out. A formula works. It can always be fined tuned to get better just as I have done but it will never change. One plus one, no matter how you look at it, no matter the language or even culture, will ALWAYS give you the same answer.

When you put sugar into a lemonade mix, everyone will require a different amount to meet their specific taste. It's still the same mixture, just how much of what. From a small business to a fortune 500 business, my formula works. To prove a valid point about paying attention, I had a client once ask me "How can you say you are the king of marketing without even a degree in this field?". A piece of paper only proves you can read a book.

You almost always have two choices in life no matter the situation. You want a car that looks nice that you can drive sometimes? Or do you want a dependable everyday vehicle that looks decent enough? I don't go with either option. I am providing you with a third, very rare option. The option that gives you exotic looks, dependability and it works every day.

I wouldn't do it, if it wasn't me. Plain and simple, I am a natural, and if it didn't make sense, it isn't me. What I'm saying is that I don't follow beliefs. Somehow my mind and my body are in tune with what just works. I could almost fill an entire book with ideas that people told me would not work, only to show you that when I do them, they turn out better than anticipated. I could practice all day long, but I know based upon facts and science, that no matter what I do, no matter how hard I try, I could never become an NFL legend, much less take a hit from a defensive lineman. There are things we truly know about ourselves and things we don't. But I do know with the exact same knowledge that I have the capability and skillset to spot a potential great, that could become an NFL legend. I could pick that person based upon proven and known facts. Stats, precision game play, and potential. You have that capability to do so as well. You know exactly what to do. Take a small step back and look at your business from an outside perspective. Tell yourself, "This is where it is" and then say, "This is where I want it to be." Now call the necessary play, put the right people in position, and get your business where it needs to be. I'm sorry to say, but sometimes people need to be moved to a different part of the business for improved overall performance, and sometimes just completely cut from the team.

There are no feelings in business. You wouldn't put shitty gas in your Rolls Royce now just because the gas station attendant appears to look a certain way and it may help him out somehow by doing so. No. That could potentially destroy something very, very, important. All bullshit aside, some businesses use that as a tactic. Making you feel bad so that you donate money for their cause or buy from them. Not because you want to, but because now their marketing ploy is playing on one's emotions. And guess what, it works! You donate that $0.20 a day to help a starving child and so do 5 million other people. Do you really think they are helping as many people as you think? Not even close. Those countries and the children there are still in great peril. But you keep donating that $0.20 a day. You are being blinded by emotion for a moment and it's actually terrible because although your intentions are great, they are using marketing for its intended purpose. To get your money.

What about the kid who is at the freeway offramp that you give change to daily along with 25,000 other people who do the same thing? His college tuition is being paid for, his rent, and his brand spanking new Camaro, all because of a little bit of marketing manipulation. You want facts. This is as real as it gets. Not some bullshit, get rich quick scheme. I do in fact work hard. And my hard work, makes you a lot of money. Think about that.

Chapter 29

This comes up quite a bit. "I don't have a big office, I don't look like a big professional company, therefore I will not succeed and people will not take me serious." Well, guess what. You're right. If you think like that then that's exactly what will happen. Remember this? Jeff Bezos and his wife started Amazon in their garage. Go out to your garage right now if you have one, or shed, or whatever space you may have available that is not being used for any reason aside from storage. I guarantee that with the right angle, you can take this space you have and turn it into your office for your next big idea. It's not what you have or don't have, it's your attitude. I started a multi-million-dollar marketing company from my prison cell. You have a computer, a laptop, an iPad, or even just your cell phone? Well guess what, you can plant your butt at your dining room table, or even your couch and be just as successful. Be glad no one has to smuggle in anything for you to use. Think about where it would have been hidden.

My son is just a few days from his 20th birthday. I spoke with him on the phone today. Being in Federal Prison you don't get to use the phone much and when you do, it's limited to 15 minutes per call and no more than twice a day. To me, these calls are crucial. But this specific call was not what I had expected. Normally he asks if I'm okay. He usually asks about updates on fights, riots and other issues so he can be supportive. But today happened to be a much more important conversation. A father and son conversation, that, believe it or not also was based on a form of marketing. How can a parent/child conversation be deep and be about marketing? Well, just like this. He started to ask me about all the nice things we had prior to my arrest and the Feds taking everything. He asked me, "Why did you have so many motorcycles, cars, and all kinds of random stuff?" I flew airplanes for fun, drove race cars, and pretty much did what I wanted when I wanted for one reason and one reason only. To show my son that he too, with hard work, could have whatever he wanted. No matter what obstacles are in your way, pretty much anything you want to do can still be done. I work hard, I get everything in life I go after and I stay focused. So, my son told me, "Dad, none of my friends have parents who have and do the things that you do." I asked him, "Son, do your friends' parents work nearly as hard as I do?" And he quickly understood why we had the life that we did. And to you, the reader, everything I have worked for is a form of marketing.

Advice can be like quicksand, or helium. One will pull you down and get you stuck, and the other can lift you so high it makes you nervous. I'd rather not sink. When I look to someone for advice there are specific things I'm looking for as far as proof goes to see if the advice is sound. Does that make sense? Is what this person telling me, logical? Does it seem realistic? Or does it sound completely bat shit crazy? Does it sound outside the box and exciting? It better make sense on some level. I don't know about you but I'm not taking any advice regarding eating and exercising from someone who is severely overweight and eats junk food all day long. No way. I'm going to someone who looks like they are preparing for a bodybuilding competition because they are dedicated and clear-cut proof that what they say is true. The results are right in front of me. If I am looking for advice on marriage and want a long, strong committed relationship, I don't care if you have more degrees than a thermostat, I am going to that couple for advice who has 5 kids, have been married for twenty plus years, because that's proof. You know they've been through some shit together and as a family. You know in your mind and your heart they haven't always had a simple life. They know exactly what good days and bad days look like. Because to have been together that long and have that many kids, is first of all insane, but incredibly difficult work. I go straight to where the proof is.

Chapter 30

When I pull up in something flashy and exotic, it often times reminds me of when I was a kid, back at Barnes & Noble, bugging the guy in the nice suit and expensive car. Why? Because that's the first moment in my life I visually saw what I wanted. And now I am there. When I get off my chopper, or out of my new muscle car, or you see pictures of me flying airplanes, people now come up to me and ask the same question I used to ask others. What do you do? Want to know what I do? I don't blow them off, I engage. I energize and motivate them to want those things as well. My conversations themselves are a form of marketing. People will say, "Man, I wish I could have a life like that", and I always tell them the same thing. "You can, because I do."

When you get the right advice, and it fits with what you are looking for, and everything lines up, when you see the lifestyle you want, the vacations you want to take, and all the things you want to buy and do with and for your family then stop. It can be yours. All of it. If you feel right now that your life is subpar, it sucks, you're tired of the same shit every single day, and your life is going absolutely nowhere, then let's change it. But how will you do it? How dedicated are you? Do you want to be as successful as you want to breathe? Do you need success like you need food? That's when everything will change. Don't quit what you're doing, just quit doing it the way you're doing it.

I see potential in millions of people everywhere I go. There's more talent out there than you can imagine. The problem is a lot of people don't see it in themselves. Sell yourself to you. Make yourself believe that you are capable and you will be. If you tell yourself, "Yes I can", then you can. Market you, to yourself. Because it all starts with you. Once you figure out just how you operate, both externally and internally, then you're ready to begin marketing to others.

Why do I always pull up in something flashy or wear something that people comment on? Because if I just start approaching people everywhere telling them about marketing without any immediate visual interest, then I just come off as a crazy person spouting stuff. Which even if it does make sense and is accurate, our eyes don't allow us to get past that due to how our brains operate. Your food could taste great, but if it looks like it came out of a dumpster, would you actually eat it? No way. Most would not. We are after appeal, visual stimulation.

For instance, no one is really a fan of people riding their bikes around your neighborhood, early in the morning, pounding on doors, spouting the word of their God. But in nearly every single time of need, what do most people do? They pray to a God. Even in religion and belief. Human beings are stuck on convenience. "Make my life convenient" is what we all want every single day. The new cell phone that just came out might cost $1,200, but it makes my life convenient therefore I must have it. So back to my awesome stuff that people are always commenting on, "Hey, nice car," "Nice motorcycle," "Nice suit." My response is always the same to everyone. "Thank you." And then I immediately follow it up with, "Would you like to know how I got it?" Sounds crazy right? But virtually every single time, the reaction is somewhat of a surprise, followed by an overly excited, "YES!"

Everyone always wants to know how I got my stuff, because they see a friendly person and they are comfortable and now feel a connection. "This guy isn't so bad. He's friendly, approachable, and social. I'd like to be more like that. I want a positive and outgoing life like that." And immediately you are learning about marketing. Marketing is all around us. People who are even religious try to talk to me about God in a marketing way. "How can you not believe in God? Take a look around at all the beautiful stuff on earth." I'm not saying you should or should not be religious and in no way shape or form am I kicking the message to you, but just saying marketing is in everything, everywhere. And your job as a business owner is to identify it. You identify the marketing that you need to do for your business, and I'll bring you the clients and customers which will in turn boost your revenue. I've often been on my way to a meeting or running an errand just to strike up a conversation along the way with a stranger who has stopped to ask me a question. And I will gladly take 20 minutes out of my day, sometimes longer to talk to them about marketing. I can't tell you how many entrepreneurs and social media influencers I have met along the way. If you have questions, I can help. There are even times where I've went to put gas in my car and the person at the next pump comments on my vehicle and a week later, they are messaging me to say thanks because they made an extra five to ten thousand dollars the previous week based on something I mentioned they should try.

When it's my first time in a business, it's brand new to me. Even if you've been there for 10 years, or your product has been on the market a long time, or it's just come out, if it's new to me, it's going to be new to millions of other people. I tell people, "Wow. You have got to get this product out there; more people need to know about your business or your product." "You're a model? How come you don't have 100K or nearly 1 million followers yet?" "I don't know" is the most common response I get. But I do. I know exactly how to get your business out there in front of millions of people. Because that's what I do. And no, I'm not talking about advertising, I'm talking about all the people who are really interested in what you already have or already doing. All the people who love what you do but don't know you exist. I will bring all these people to your social media pages as well as your websites.

An inmate had a great idea to help other inmates with outside resources. In prison, we rely on friends and family to get things done for us, but these people work and have busy schedules. We put together a business plan which was to include in this program a way to hire a personal assistant on the outside to help with everything from ordering books to have them sent in, down to study materials, along with other items that we are allowed to have in prison, but don't have access to obtaining without help from friends and family. His ideas could help hundreds of thousands of incarcerated individuals. As a matter of fact, as of this moment right now there are 2.2 million people locked up in the United States. For this service, the market is fairly large. He told me, "I don't know how to market this, but I know this is a solution to a major national problem." He's right. His business plan provides a solution to a need where options are limited. I broke down a full marketing plan for him. He has a good test market here with over 1,000 prisoners who all said, "Yes, I need this program and would use it regularly." The research is done. Now to bring all his clients to him. That's where I come in. I explained to him how I can bring nearly all inmates in this country to what you do. There is a demand for his service and a massive group of people who both need and want it. And I have the skills to bring them all directly to him. They trust him, because he is them. He needs the same things they do. And they all know he is in the same exact position as all of them. It's a no brainer.

So, if you are brand new to this, you have a business idea, a new business, a product or some type of service, let's market the shit out of it. Your experience isn't the issue. Just know who to bring in.

Chapter 31

The hair care industry is massive. Every single day, in every city, everywhere around the world, someone, if not hundreds maybe even thousands, are in salons getting their hair cut, styled, and/or even dyed. Due to legal reasons as well as an NDA I signed; I can only divulge so much information regarding this next bit. I'm currently consulting on a project that will in fact change the salon industry as we all know it. A product that no one has thought to make. I've been discussing this with one of the most knowledgeable hair stylists in the country. She has taught at beauty schools and has more experience in the industry than anyone I've ever met. Why is she discussing this product with me? I have no hair, and know absolutely nothing about her industry. However, I know the consumers and I recognize the problem that this must-have product solves. And no, it's not a hair dye or some hair care product. Everyone knows there's an abundant amount of that stuff on the market. This particular item is beneficial to salons, will be noticeable by all, and will make a visual statement to all salons depending on the color they choose. But either way, it's a game changer for the industry. She asked me, "How do I get the salons nationwide to know about the product?" That's the beautiful part. With this item, it can increase sales for the salon, more clientele, and an incentive as to why people need to come to their salons. As soon as the patent is complete, the injection mold is finished, a bold color choice is made, she will then give one to a few major salons. She has hired me to bring everyone together who understands the problem that this fixes. My company's job is to put all of these people onto that product. Yes. I even know how to get clients and customers for items they don't even know exist yet.

The formula to my marketing can literally find any customer for any item or service that you have. Wondering where or whom your demographic is? Does it already exist? Maybe it does and you have no idea where to locate them. I do.

I study business like I'm a chemist or something. I break everything down to its most basic form to see how it works. How will it react? What will the feedback be? There is in fact a science to all of this.

Recently, I took a group of people who had minimum wage jobs. Some even worked at Walmart, some worked at Target, and even one that never actually had a job. I asked if they would let me try an experiment with them to prove they were worth at least $200 per hour. (Of course, everything was above board and completely legal). Some were skeptical. Some just gave me blank stares and did not believe me. I told them, if they listened to my rules and guidelines for this particular project, and followed everything exactly as laid out, just try, no questions asked, within two weeks you will be making nearly $200 per hour. Well, it didn't go exactly as planned. Some made just under $400 per hour. Some exceeded beyond what they even thought was possible. And to be perfectly honest, every single one of them had never done anything in this field ever. They were all on the same level of experience which was zero. When this project was over, they all asked me how did they manage to do so well. I explained that when it comes to marketing, all I did was show people a side of them that they themselves didn't know they had. Many ended up quitting their jobs immediately and continued to work even harder. I showed them how the general public saw them, and then everything changed. Marketing is truly magical and can in fact change your entire life. I've helped many people change their entire life for the better with my skills and techniques.

This all led to me becoming the best damn marketing specialist and creating the most efficient global social media marketing company.

I walked into the vehicle wrap company that eventually did my truck. My truck had a 10" lift on it and was a quad cab. I know what you're thinking. And no. I'm 6'1", 202lbs, and absolutely have no need to compensate for anything. I just like to drive over things. Being as big as this truck was, it would take a lot of material to wrap it entirely. But it was worth it. Had I paid out of pocket I would have spent nearly $5,000 for the complete job. The initial custom carbon fiber wrap, the massive chrome overlay for the company logo, it was amazing! But the way I did pay for it was through marketing. I explained that due to me being a government contractor, my truck was going to be seen everywhere. And it was. All over the west coast as well as all over social media. And every time I posted anything, photos, TV commercials, interviews both on TV and radio, I mentioned their company. This led to them making nearly twenty times more than I would've paid for it out of pocket. Needless to say, it was a good job. I was happy with their product and they were happy with all the extra money I had made them. Even if I was out and about eating, at a stoplight, or just wherever and someone said, "Hey! That's a nice truck. I love the wrap!" I would immediately tell them to pull out their phone and look up this company on social media and follow them. "Let them know I referred you!" It's a win win. This was towards the beginning of my social media mastery.

For my next marketing adventure, I didn't even see this one coming. I was out and about one day in my truck of course, when I spotted a chopper dealership (custom motorcycles). I decided to check it out as I've always had an affinity for motorcycles. I had been in the door maybe less than ten minutes before it caught my attention. It practically screamed, "Take me home tonight!" And yes, we all love Eddie Money. I fell in love immediately. The rear tire on this thing was wide enough to hold up the bike all by itself. And the raked-out forks were just long enough to make any U-turn an easy eight-point turn. It was like looking at a wild horse and telling yourself, "Yeah, I can break this thing." I skipped the salesman and went directly to the owner of this small chopper dealer. Pulled him aside and began to make him an offer. Before I could say much, he interrupted and asked, "Is that your big ass truck out there?" My response to everyone was the same. "Yes, it is! This is America and we love big, badass shit!" Then he asked what the business was that had been displayed on my truck. And that's when I knew I had him. You can tell almost immediately if someone is a gun fanatic. Just like you can tell who isn't. This guy was all about guns. However, he too was a convicted felon, with a very successful business. I showed him pictures of the weapons I designed for the military and he was soon smiling from ear to ear. After a short discussion he asked, "How can I help you?"

To be courteous and not offensive I calmly responded with, "Actually, I was wondering if you'd allow me to help you." We headed to his office and I explained my interest in this particular chopper. He said it wasn't ready as it still needed some paint. I wanted it just the way it was. Raw! I spent fifteen minutes explaining to him what it was I would like to do for him. "You'll give me the bike, I'll sell at least 10 others for you." He was standing to make over $180,000 off this agreement. I'll promote it. Everywhere I ride, everyone will know exactly where I got it from. It will be used in photos and other advertisements for my weapons business throughout social media. His initial response was "Hmm." Then he followed it up with what seemed to be a tiny concern which I greatly appreciated. He then said, "Do you have someone who can drive your truck home?" I told him, "Of course." Then he handed me a brand-new helmet, the keys to the bike, and a nice solid handshake. We met for a few drinks later that evening to discuss more marketing strategies that I could help him with.

Remember, when your business gives me something, whether it's a product or service, it's not fee. I'm paying you for it at a significantly higher price than anyone else. Because I really want it. Because I choose to market your business, I can now stream additional revenue that you previously did not have. On top of that, you can now write this off as a business expense. Why would I do this? Why would I spend the time helping your business succeed and make you up to an extra six, maybe even seven figures annually? Because you made me care. You provided me with something which shows you care. You believe in yourself and the value of your product and are open to the idea of outside help to build up your product and brand. Plus, I enjoy it.

Seeing a business flourish is what I thrive on. I love helping all types of businesses. It's a challenge that I wake up to conquer every day. Not only is it a write-off for your business, but it's a new business relationship. You're investing in yourself. And when it comes down to it, it's affordable. With a one-time transaction, versus a monthly one it also saves you a ton of money on both market research as well as marketing. There is absolutely nothing more profitable than direct marketing. Some companies spend a fortune on customer acquisition, when AEY MARKETING's formula guarantees each acquisition may only be pennies. Of course, you could hire a celebrity to wear and pose with your product, or endorse it on a commercial, but then you're putting it out there in hopes that it will gain and attract business. My formula simply brings it. No hoping, wondering, or even guessing. My marketing strategy is numbers that cannot be falsified because you (the business owner), see them for yourself.

Chapter 32

It didn't end there. Soon came a suit designer who gave me a suit, then another. Then came the jewelry and other really neat shit. I'm waiting for an alcohol endorsement. I'm kidding. I'll probably start my own brand. Afterall, anything I get behind and market does better than just well.

The first time I was approached to work for a company to solely do marketing for them was a nice gesture. However, my counter offer was much better. If I have the ability to grow sales for an individual business, I would much rather be a part of it. So, I offered 2%. For 2% of the annual net revenue, I would spend 365 days a year doing nothing but driving clients and customers to an organization that I am now a physical part of. Why not? The more I put into it, the more we all make. It was a simple yes on their part. The beautiful part of it all is you now have someone doing this fulltime without having to worry about a monthly bill. You've now added value to your company. And it comes with all the free marketing input on the side that you would like. Suggestions? Questions? Comments? You now have your own in-house marketing specialist to help your current team maximize its profits.

You could go out and hire a consultant, and spend more than you would out of pocket, than having a solid team working with your business on a regular basis. You also wouldn't get the dedication and appreciation for what you do.

I once sold someone's house who wasn't even interested in selling it until they saw the offer I was able to put in front of them. After that, recently I purchased a banked owned townhouse, put some money into it and sold it for nearly double just to see if I could. The realtor said I was out of my mind to list it for the price I did. Within two weeks of being the highest priced property of its kind in the area, it sold. And the realtor wanted to know how I did it. I explained my entire marketing process, but the realtor thought I was crazy, but he admitted that it worked.

Just like life, there isn't always an explanation as to why things go the way they do, or why some things work out, they just do. I'm one of those people. When it comes to business, no matter the field, I just see things. Not like some psychic, but I take everything in, about the business, the structure, the goals, the people who work there, and I just see what others don't. I see the big picture, not just the two-, three-, or five-year goal. I see the entire picture. My potential when it comes to marketing is indescribable.

What are your hobbies? Probably normal shit, right? Skiing? Boating? Golfing? Drawing? Maybe even reading. One of my favorites is getting people to quit their aimless jobs. Now you may ask yourself, why on earth would someone try and get someone else to quit their job that they "love" so much, a job they work 100 hours a week at, and make just enough money to survive? I'll tell you why. Because they are the people who want more out of life. The ones who work harder than they have to with no reward. Living check to check and making just enough to cover bills is not living. That's surviving. Nearly struggling to survive. No relaxation, no enjoyment. This is not the kind of person who should be employed by someone else. This person should be running their own business. If you worked this hard for someone else to barely get by imagine what you could do if it was your business you worked this hard for.

I've walked into countless businesses and told myself; "I'm going to get a deserving person to walk out and quit their job right now." For the pure benefit of seeing them succeed. Believe it or not, a lot of people are stuck because they are terrified. Stuck in the most general way. They aren't terrified because their job is dangerous. They aren't even terrified of their bosses. They are terrified to walk up to someone and be honest. "I quit." are the most unsupportive words when placed together in a statement. No one wants to wants to quit anything. In fact, as a child your parents probably drilled into you. "Don't start something and then quit at it." Here's a great example. When I was a kid, I played little league baseball for four years. I wasn't the best and I wasn't the worst. Some said I had serious potential. I just stopped enjoying it after four years. I asked my mom if I could stop playing and she said, "No." She told me she didn't think I should quit. She kept telling me to stick with it. "Stick with what?" I'm going to be perfectly honest with you. I asked her how long then must I play before I can stop so it's not called quitting. She then decided I was being a smartass and attempted to ground me. That wasn't going to happen.

There are two kinds of quitting. But no one will tell you any different. There's the bad kind of "I QUIT," when you are just lazy and probably shouldn't have started the project to begin with, because you know deep down you suck at it, you have no feelings involved, and you had no intention on even getting halfway through it from the beginning. Then there's the positive "I quit." The, "I've put myself out there and gave 110% and I'm just not happy with myself or my life. I'm stressed out every day, have thought about assaulting someone regularly due to my job, sick of not getting anywhere no matter how hard I work, and have absolutely not a care in world regarding the company I work for." That's the positive, "I quit." Sounds kind of nuts, I know. But this is where that becomes the right thing to do. In this situation you are not in fact quitting anything. You're taking control of your life and making it better. Believe me, this "I QUIT" is probably safer for you and your co-workers. You know the term "going postal?" I believe those people should've taken the positive "I quit" approach. It would've saved them a lot of grief as well as made a much safer workplace for countless others. This is your health and your life. Never let anyone dictate what you need to do for you. When you quit, it's a positive thing. It means you quit being subservient, you quit wasting time and letting life wastefully go by. You quit taking no for an answer. You quit being not successful. Now it's time to stand up. Not to someone else, but stand up to yourself. When you can do that, you can release all that built up negativity that's been building up for who knows how long. It's like working out. You may hate doing it, but when you're done and you're taking your post workout shower, either alone, or with someone else, you will always say the same thing. "I'm glad I did it." You feel a million times better. Except with this, it's a life changer for you and everyone around you.

Speaking of quitting. Today I spoke with a corrections officer in regards to signing up for classes or how to go about teaching a class to get time knocked off my sentence. He cut me off midway and told me he has thought about quitting his job for quite some time. For nearly 20 minutes he explained how he was so stressed out and how he feels he has been wasting his life and was hoping to get more out of it. My response? I said "Do it." His immediate response was fear. Fear of the unknown. Fear of success. We live with fear, we work with fear, we work through fear, we make decisions based on fear, most of our lives are based on solely how afraid we are that things may go badly. By taking a chance on something positive, it will not rid you of your fear, but it sure as hell will make life more enjoyable and fear just a little bit less. He asked me how I could be so sure. He asked why I was in prison and I was still so confident and sure of myself. So, I explained to him who I was and my story. And how being exceptionally great at marketing led me straight to Federal Prison. He realized I wasn't a drug dealer or doing anything illegal and began to ask me several business questions. I explained how I had become a really big weapons defense contractor for the U.S. Government and started out with just $45,000. He was able to google some of the weapons I designed and built for military and law enforcement agencies. I spoke to him about the fear that encapsulates all of us. Shit, I damn near raised my son alone for a majority of his life. I was terrified every damn day. But I did it. And you can as well.

So, we spoke for about an hour. Even told him I'm writing this very book that you are reading. Shot him some serious tips and saw that he was able to understand them. He explained further that he wanted to quit his setback in life to pursue something more fulfilling. I asked him if he had made a list of ideas. Here's where the fear crept back in. He responded with a, "No". He said, "By writing it down, it brings the realization of what I am doing in my life to my attention and I don't want to admit that this job is defeating me." What a deep answer. So, I gave him the task to make a list of what he would like to do even if he didn't feel it was realistic.

Chapter 33

The first step to success is exactly that. Just a step. Not a leap, not a bound, and doesn't even have to be quicker than a speeding bullet. It's just one simple step. We've gotten to the point in society where we track every single thing that we do. We wear Fitbits to track our actual steps. And what's that magical number someone came up with that we all try and accomplish every day? 10,000 steps! Holy shit! That's a lot. Who came up with that? Seriously though. 10,000 steps are so many. 10,000 of anything is a lot. It's kind of overwhelming, right? If you ask me, one step seems so much easier. Especially if that one single step can change your entire life. You try 10,000 steps every day and how much of an impact are you making? Are you seeing the results you want? Most likely not. But one step in the right direction will in fact change all of that. And once you've taken that first step, everything else after that is so much easier. Have you ever tried to take off your pants without removing your shoes? Yes. We've all done this at some point in our life. We struggle and realize at some point when a shoe is stuck in your pant leg, "I should have taken that one step to take my shoes off first." Now you begin to struggle, waste precious time, and you end up starting the entire process all over again just to do what you should have to begin with. And how much easier is it? So much that we ask ourselves as we are doing it, "Why didn't I just do this from the beginning?" You don't have to be a genius to figure this out. But sometimes it helps when you're not so close to the project.

"When you take a step back from the picture, it's easier to see the frame."

I would say that it makes more sense to be able to see what it is you are doing, but take a look at Helen Keller, Ray Charles, Stevie Wonder, and many others. They couldn't see shit and yet changed the world. Although they couldn't see the big picture visually, it was felt around the world. If they can do it, so can you. Marketing comes from having a very strong belief in something. In yourself and what it is you are capable of. Make that list and change your world.

Marketing is so powerful that it makes people not only become dreamers, but also believers. When you were a kid, what did you dream of becoming when you grew up? Was it an astronaut because of that super cool ass space suit? A cop or even a fire fighter? Marketing is involved in your life at your earliest stages of development. Now let me ask you a serious question. Did you become, or end up doing what you always dreamed of? If not, then why? Something made you want to do it. Something gave you that desire just by seeing it. And then poof. It vanished. It's never too late to make your life the way it should be. We all get side tracked in life. However, by maintaining focus on yourself and your goals, also sets you up for the level of happiness you can truly achieve. Think about it. While you are stressed out at your dead-end job, making someone else's dreams come true, what is it doing for you? It sure isn't helping you start the business you've always dreamed about, or the service you can provide to others.

I once interviewed a professional gardener. Yes, this is real. And no, it's not as exciting as it sounds. But it was sure profound as fuck. I had to interview her because I had heard of this, but didn't know exactly how real it was or even exactly what it was that she actually did. I was under the impression that either you grew stuff, or you didn't. And either you were amazing at it, or you just sucked. Turns out she dropped a huge knowledge bomb on me. You hire her to come to your home, apartment, loft, or wherever the hell you intend on beginning your garden. She covers everything from prime location, to what you will need, even down to what you can expect to grow well (whether it's indoor or not), not grow well, purpose of your garden down to the very last detail. Once everything is planned out, she sets everything up with you and walks you through every step of the process from beginning to the time you plant your seeds. How much to water, what nutrients to add (depending on what you're growing), what not to add, and how often.

It blew my mind at how much is involved in this process. She explained that hundreds of thousands of people love gardening. Many want a new garden, but few know exactly where to begin or what's actually needed for their particular one. Those who plow forward (no pun intended), without the necessary knowledge and skills often realize things aren't working out as intended. It's not that they aren't capable, it's just that they may have missed a step or two and due to a simple misstep, the end results cause them to feel as if they can't actually do it. It's not their fault. They aren't informed to the point where they can start properly. So, she said, "Many have become hopeless and turn what could be a beautiful, healthy hobby into an issue that they carry onto other things in life." Interesting. Gardening, is a delicate process. It can be quite fruitful and very empowering if done with the appropriate amount of information required. Clearly, she loves to garden. It changed her entire life. And it's changed the lives of many. She explained that once people were shown the proper way, they were more confident in general. Felt more capable and had a new sense of pride. By her knowing how to help someone take the first step in the right direction, which for her was easy to teach, she had given people a new connection in life that brought on a healthy and more positive attitude. When asked, "Why?" She simply stated, "Some people just need help with the first step. It's not that you can't do something, it's just if you don't have the proper tools to handle the task at hand, things can seem incredibly difficult."

Chapter 34

I naturally progressed in marketing. I spent many, many nights and countless hours developing my formula to market the way I do. I mastered real, global social media marketing. I bring people direct to your business, who are already interested in your product or service.

Not only have I taken the first step towards everything I've ever wanted to do, but I have in fact mastered the art of marketing in ways that many wish they knew how to do. I'm not asking you to become a marketing guru or to even get you to understand how it works, just that you ultimately understand that more clients and customers equate to more revenue, which results in more money, in your pocket. This is what I do. And this is what I would like to do for you. Why would I work with celebrities and pro athletes, and then take everything I have learned to help others? Because someone needs to. It's only right that everyone has the same opportunities to succeed. Not only will I do your marketing the right way, but I will go through your entire social media to ensure your business, your service, or your products are presented accordingly for maximization. I will do everything available that I am able to do in order for you to succeed. Just like the gardening professional. I will go through every step, show you what's needed, what's not needed, and ensure that you understand the purpose of your business from your customers angle, so that you can maximize the number or customers and clients brough to you. The better I am at what I do, the more money you make. And together we will do great! Have a YouTube channel that you want millions to see? Done! Decided you'd like to become a social media influencer but need a massive fanbase? Done! Maybe you're a local mom and pop business, but would like to expand for your children and possibly grandchildren, so they may one day have something that's passed along? Done!

Someone a while back did in fact rip off a movie line and told me "If you build it, they will come." This absolutely couldn't be anything farther from the truth. Now, if you build it, they'll have a place to come to, but how in the hell are they going to know it's there? Or that it even exists? Marketing!

"Just because you have something amazing or even life changing, doesn't mean customers will fall from the sky into your cash register. In fact, if no one knows about it, you'll lose your entire investment and quite possibly everything you've worked for and become bankrupt within one year."

Okay. Maybe not entirely that aggressive, but pretty damn close. I've seen it happen. I asked a restaurant once, to allow me to advertise for them, absolutely FREE simply because I loved their food so much. The owner said no and refused permission for me to do so. She told me she would get customers on her own simply because the food was that delicious. Not going to lie. The food was amazing! And man do I miss that restaurant.

Believe it or not, this is something that happens quite frequently. You have a great idea or invention, possibly an exceptional service. Well guess what? We have to tell everyone about it. And I mean everyone. Don't get hung up on who you tell, just tell everyone. I know millions of people who know about the Kardashians. Doesn't mean we like them or even buy their stuff, but we all know who they are. I've never purchased the smart-clapper, or actually know anyone else who has, but we all know what it is. Again, the more people who know, the better off your business will be in the long run.

As human beings, marketing is literally ingrained into our DNA. If you don't believe it, take a look around. When someone buys a car, they put new rims on it because of how it will make it look. Women wear an excessive amount of makeup, not because they are all ugly, but because of the way they feel it makes them look. Let's face it, almost everyone cares about the way things look. From your clothes down to your food. Would you eat a meal that looks as if it just arrived from a dumpster? I'd hope not. Do people (society in general) not get leery if someone is dressed more ragged than most or hasn't seemed to have had a shower in some time?

Your home, your image, your fiends even. As sad as it may seem, some people actually pick their friends based upon their appearance. This isn't news to anyone as we all watch reality TV shows. And some may prefer to hang out with what some may consider less desirable than most in order to make themselves look better, in their opinion. These are many studies that have been done on this matter. Which in itself is pretty damn sad. Looks are everything in today society. And Hollywood definitely makes sure to drive this point across without holding back. Even the way we speak is marketing. We say things like "watch" what you say, and would you "look" at that! Aesthetics are everything. As it should be. We feel as a society, the better something looks the more inviting it may be. People spend more time ensuring something appears a certain way, more than they spend time doing literally anything else in their lives. Let me be perfectly clear. There is nothing wrong with this mentality. We are human beings, and to be social is part of our genetic makeup. We were designed to engage with others. Hence why we love entertainment. Would you rather listen to your favorite artist in your bedroom alone? Or would you rather go to a concert with your friends and 50,000 screaming fans to watch a live show, drink, and have an amazing visual performance by your favorite band? Exactly what I though. As human beings, we are a business. What is our business? Apparently any and everything that catches our eye or is appealing in some form or another. We love seeing new things so much that not seeing something is equally as fun.

My friend owns and operates an upscale restaurant called BLACKOUT. It is a nice restaurant that no one will ever see. It's crazy. The waiters wear NVGs (Night Vision Goggles) in order to hold your hand and guide you to your seat. You can't even see your hand in front of your face. We are talking pitch fucking black. You lock your phones in a locker in the lobby, sign a waiver and pick the type of taste you are interested in experiencing for your meal. And in case you were wondering, there are no knives at the tables. But people are ranting and raving about this place and have been for quite some time. A place that no one can see, that people are desperately wanting to be at. Right?

Chapter 35

My son often asks me, "Dad, if you could do everything all over again, would you have done anything different?" Absolutely not. As an international arms dealer, competition can be dangerous. I was so competitive that it landed me in Federal Prison. And I mean it. I am solely in prison because my marketing skills are so good, that it pissed off the wrong person.

An individual that I cannot name, was so upset with how quickly I was growing and expanding that this person called in a solid, and had me completely wiped out. It was told to me explicitly one day, that you don't go from being a nobody in this game to negotiating weapons deals with the Secret Service, without pissing off a competitor in the process. Well, I did. And I did. To the point where the government stepped in and took every single thing I had without so much as a warrant. Normally, the government is required to have things like warrants and other documents to seize everything you have. Not in my case. And most of the time, they've got to charge you with some sort of crime to put you in Federal Prison. Not in my case. Somehow, the government violated every single thing it says it stands for, just to put me in federal custody. All because I'm that damn good at marketing. Granted in your line of work, that won't happen. The worst I've ever seen is a major company comes along, buys out your company, and then shuts it down if they feel it can be a threat to their primary revenue stream.

The federal prosecutors told me that for wasting their time, (meaning there was no direct evidence implicating me in any wrongdoing or breaking any laws) they would attempt to give me the maximum time, take away my good time, and make me suffer as much as possible. And boy did they try and keep true to their promise. Not only did I not get any sort of pre-trial release hearing, not a single motion was filed on my behalf, but I in fact got nearly an extra year added on top of my sentence, after I was sentenced. Nope. It wasn't another charge and no, I did not get in any sort of trouble while in prison. Someone, again, can't mention any names, decided to say that my first year in Federal Prison did not count towards my sentence. So, while everyone else who was locked up allegedly for drugs, guns, and other crazy shit, were able to get out early, go to a halfway house, and even home confinement, I wasn't so much even allowed to get a job or take any classes to get time reduced. Oh, they wanted me bad. And they got me. Breaking me wasn't going to happen. I don't scare easily and you can't persuade me to do something I don't want to do. And due to the way I was raised, nothing, I mean absolutely nothing, scares me other than my own mother. I am not afraid of anything. So, whatever the U.S. Government was attempting to do, did nothing to me but place me on an extended vacation. I didn't even have to worry about any bills. Zero stress, aside from daily fights, and stabbings. And if you were raised by my mother, then you would know. Bring on the fights, riots, and stabbings. I'll take them by the truckload. Doesn't bother me one bit. That was day camp compared to being raised by my mom. And I mean that in the best way possible. She prepared me for life unlike anything you could ever imagine. I have fought my entire life to survive and succeed, and have been damn good at it.

Would I want someone who is going to do a half ass job for me, or someone who will bust their ass to succeed? I want the person who is relentless, who doesn't give up, who would stop at nothing, to ensure we both become successful. Marketing is all about skill. Sometimes when you're too good at something, people don't like it. Especially if it means they are going to lose out on something financially because you are better than they are. No one likes money being taken out of their pocket. But you're not taking it out of their pockets, or anywhere else they should be concerned with. When I make money for someone, it's because their customers want that money to go to them and not someone else. Yes, a lot has to do with my marketing capabilities, but part of that has to do your products and service. So, screw the competition. They're mad because they can't do as well and that's just natural. But instead of complaining about it, they have the equal ability to hire me, just as you're about to do.

Will we work for everyone? No. Because some of you have the inability to be humble. But for you, the person reading this, knows it's better to grow than not to, because it equates to you making more money. Yes, you. You know what it takes to move forward while the other is stuck, constantly complaining and wondering why he or she can't expand, and find the clients he or she needs just as you are about to. Winners don't bitch and complain. We just get up; we do what's required and then some. We push the envelope. And when we do bitch, it's because we want to do more than we already have done. But we step to the plate and crush our opponents because we have what it takes.

Who cares that I am an international arms dealer, or that I'm now a convicted felon? Not a single person who really matters cares anything about this. You know why? Because I don't cut corners and I don't cheat at anything I do. I simply work my ass off as I have always done. And great competition will always upset someone else. If you don't find anyone bothered or upset with you for how hard you have been working, then you're not working hard enough. If everyone seems to like you, then you are doing something entirely wrong. Of course, it's good to be nice, courteous and loyal, but you know just as well as I do that none of those things will pay the bills.

When you have nothing, you think love will get you on the bus? Not a fat chance in hell. Feelings and emotions can't pay bills. Your power company doesn't give two shits who lives in your home, how old or young they may be, or what ailments anyone in your family may have. They want their payment or your power is getting shut off.

When it comes to those who care, my favorite is the friend, or "supportive" person that says shit like, "Maybe you should consider doing things this way," or, "Maybe you shouldn't do this," or, "Maybe you should do that." Now I don't know about you, but I find it fascinating that there is always someone willing to throw in their two fucking cents when it comes to telling someone else how to run their life. Especially when you're kind of a piece of shit yourself. And then I would stop and ask myself before rushing judgement, "Does so and so have a legitimate reason for saying what they just said? Or has so and so had a bad experience doing something this particular way that I may be doing so?" You know, to give some sort of credibility from a personal experience. Often the answer is, "No." This person has absolutely zero experience in this field I'm in. And that's not crazy? Someone who knows absolutely jack fucking shit about something, yet wants to tell you how it should be done? Not in my house. It's one thing for someone to have experience and knowledge and entirely another for someone to be talking straight out of their ass. A lot of the time we end up finding out this is a form of jealousy or a friend, or family member who is unhappy due to your success. Don't get me wrong, some people actually do care. But that in itself is incredibly rare. We'd like to believe that when we are doing great, people want to be there to support us. Most of the time this is not the case. Ever see someone win the lottery? And suddenly they've got caring family member coming out of nowhere? Even family member they didn't know actually existed? Exactly like that. You are your number one fan. You are the President and CEO of your own fucking fan club. And only you know what works for you.

Chapter 36

"As the Marketing King, I will never tell someone about something I don't know. I know marketing. I know how to get clients, customers and increase revenue better than anyone else who has ever done this."

There are things that come naturally to me, like breathing or walking. If you took Malcolm X and Bruce Lee and combined their incredible philosophies, "By any means necessary" and "Be like water," and then you walked the fine line that paralleled those in between, you would be spot on. Do what's natural, smoothly, but work your butt off and do whatever it takes to get it done. And when you get to where you want to be, go for it! Now go and be the good person that some pretend to be, but be genuine in your ways.

Here's how good of a person I actually strived to be. Prior to my arrest, I was amidst discussing a deal with Adidas, to acquire nearly 5,000 soccer balls just to give them away to make children's lives a bit better in third world countries, simply because it was the right thing to do and I had the ability to do it. Not for publicity or recognition. Although that would've naturally come along with the project, that was not the key objective here. I could just sit back and work with celebrities and Fortune 500 companies, but that would only take me so far. I know I have the ability to help many others who need it, and it's my choice to do so. I understand that I may not be able to help everyone, but the option will be there for millions who need it.

Now, my team, my business, and my experience are available to help other businesses new and old, succeed. To do better than they have thought possible, without jumping through crazy ass hoops or having to know someone. You now know me. You know AEY MARKETING.

With Federal Prison now behind me, the biggest thing I learned is to help people. The rich don't need my help (clearly, they need someone's help, but not mine), but you might. The wealthy will always have their banks, contacts, politicians, and all their tight little circles. But now, we will have all of that and then some. At the end of the day, only you can bail yourself out of whatever mess you and your business may end up in. But we can avoid all of that now. I single handedly developed AEY MARKETING because of you. It was built for you. And designed to do something no other business has been willing to do. To make you, their priority. My priority is your success. Most marketing businesses have one goal in mind, and that's sales. They want to sell you something. In fact, they NEED to sell you something. AEY doesn't need or even want to do any of that. I don't even have anything to sell you, for what seems like once in my life. It's kind of ironic that I have spent nearly my entire life excelling at marketing by doing sales, only to get to the point where I'm not selling anything. My "sale" is simply, "Do you want to make more money?" And telling you that you don't have to be in a certain social circle to meet someone like me anymore. Now all of you, every single one of you, have direct access to AEY MARKETING. I'm not saying it's a free for all, I'm simply saying you now have a chance at something exclusive to help your business without the stress you may have previously had. Take advantage of it. You're reading this book, so clearly there's a part of you that's saying, "I want more, I want to be successful, and I want to do better than I am doing at this point." And if you are thinking like that, then you are a true business owner, an entrepreneur who doesn't want to settle, and wants to make the most out of what you are doing or involved in. You might even be a partner in an amazing company who wants more for yourself, your partners, and your employees. Well, this is it. This is how we do it.

AEY MARKETING covers everyone and everything. There is absolutely nothing out there that we can't market. And that's quite beneficial to you.

I want to cover an angle of marketing that a lot of people are curious about. Something that many question, but aren't sure how to make happen. This section is primarily for athletes, bodybuilders, and various other public figures who are after endorsement deals. Now, whether you're a college athlete, professional, a semi-professional, or in some league that you hope to advance in, popularity is key. Obviously, skill in what you do plays a factor, but you can be the most skilled at what you do and if you don't have enough fans, endorsements will fly right by you. Companies look for sales. They approach athletes who are MVPs, record breakers, gold medal earners, and other areas like this to pay them to endorse their products. The other side to this, is businesses also look at facts. Every business wants to know, "How many followers does this individual have on social media?", which in today's world is crucial. You want to be seen by more companies, and my job is to build your popularity online. It doesn't matter if you race, play tennis, wrestle, or any type of college sport and hope to go pro, a good scout will find you and get you an amazing deal.

On the way to your goal, and even afterwards, AEY MARKETING will create a fanbase for you that will help you cash in bigtime. I've helped amateur athletes land endorsement deals due to the number of followers they have. I've even personally landed a sponsorship from NAPA Auto Parts for a race team who races late model cars on a dirt track here in Las Vegas, NV. NAPA Auto Parts had no idea who they were until I made it happen. And this was an amateur league of racers. You play college softball, baseball, volleyball, race horses, or literally any sport you can think of, and I will make sure AEY boosts your fanbase to help your career out in route to endorsements and sponsorships. You don't have to wait to be the best in your league to get noticed. If you're popular, and a business thinks you're a great representative of their brand, boom, we've done it! It may even help a pro team notice you. A college or amateur athlete with a half million followers on social media will be noticed much sooner than without a fanbase. Do you surf? Skateboard? Play hockey? Then it doesn't matter. Like sports, numbers are everything. Your stats can make or break your career, and it's the same exact thing for a business. If you have the numbers they want to see, you'll start getting checks with numbers you love to see. Before a boxer goes pro, endorsements can start piling in.

"The key to marketing is to sell <u>YOU</u>."

You have fans everywhere., you just don't know it yet. A lot of people wait to hit the pros before they explore this angle. It's never too early show yourself to your potential fans as well as the rest of the world. At this point, more agents will approach you and better deals may be available. And if you're still wondering, the answer is yes! I can take a street racer and make them just as popular as any professional athlete. Crazy? Yes! But when your new endorsements start pouring in, it's even more crazy. Going from racing on the weekends, to making a few grand, to having major sponsors because of how popular you've become on social media, is one amazing thing. When companies see how big AEY has grown your fanbase, they're going to love it. This means sales. And this means way more money for you! I could go on and on about you athletes, but I think you get the point. But it doesn't end there!

For those of you who are not athletes, Olympians, racers, or stunt people hoping to get a Red Bull deal this also applies to you. How? Glad you asked. You know the Fox News anchor who just got a $2 million-dollar contract and they have the same journalism degree that you do? Well guess what? That anchor just happens to be very popular. The real estate agent who is now listing multi-million-dollar homes and not $30,000 condemned crack houses, that can also be you. How? How, what? How can that be you? How did they go from where you're at now to that level? Now you're asking the right questions. Popularity. Not because they know all the "cool people" type of popularity, but they also have very decent social media followings which allows businesses to make the decision to promote based on future sales. You're a makeup artist? Stylist? Well guess what, chances are you have a YouTube channel and with enough followers and subscribers you make a very good amount of money each month. I build your fanbase up, and now you're doing much better financially. Not only that, but businesses now want you to use their products, so they begin sending you free shit. So now, you're making even more money and getting free products on top of that. All from marketing. An insurance agent, attorney, it's all the same. Want to be able to charge more for what you do? You need the foundation to back that up. If enough people love what you do and how you do it, you have substantiated a way and reason to increase your price. I've seen popularity change companies from a mom-and-pop operation to being purchased and backed by billion-dollar corporations based on the number of followers they have on social media. These numbers are real, and they mean serious money in your pocket.

This marketing aspect eludes a lot of people. It's like when you're desperately trying to remember the name of the person or band who sings the song you've been humming all day and it's right there on the tip of your tongue, but you are still kind of stuck. And then someone comes along and says it causing you to have an, "Oh yeah!" moment. Your "Oh yeah!" moment is AEY MARKETING.

Chapter 37

Let's talk about investors. Yeah, you guys are in this too. You buy a business at a low price, you want to keep it, and make it thrive. What do you do? Most of us fix it up. Re-decorate, re-design, or even re-brand. Maybe under a new name, a new logo, and then we wait. It's a business that was once there so people should know this location is still here. It's great in theory and maybe people drive by it every day, but maybe they don't know what it has become. They know what it was and maybe that's why they are not returning to the physical location itself. Well guess what? We can now re-market this location. Let's get those people plus new ones through that door! Even if you choose to purchase land and you have goals of leasing, renting, or placing a new business on the land, people need to know it's there. Investors make money from customers and clients just like any other business, therefore people need to know those investors exist. Maybe I have a business I'd like to sell to an investor. If I know this investor exists via social media, several more offers can go directly to them.

I don't just bring the money to you. I specialize in bringing the source of the money to you. I could bring you a bottle of water, or just tap a line directly into the source of the water, and have it flow right to your location. I've worked with all sorts of people. And they all appreciate that what I am capable of doing for an A-list celebrity, I can do for them just the same. Never underestimate yourself. Every day I hear, "Oh I'm not on social media much," or "Social media isn't really for me." And if you are one of the few who work a 9-5 job at a fast-food restaurant and lovin' it, this may not be for you. But know this. Social media isn't exactly for you. It's primarily for your customer, your client, the consumer, the person who wants to pull out their credit card or debit card and pay you right this instant. It's for them. It's not just for that teenager who sits on their phone all day long, but even they help.

AEY has discovered 50,000 new followers for your business. And a handful happen to be some teenager who is on their phone 8 hours a day, who just happen to come across what you do and love it. They now have shared your business with all of their friends and family which in turn has brought you a handful of sales that you would not have, if not for my formula. What AEY MARKETING does, is create wealth. I create wealth. I am the squeaky wheel to your business. And I'll get you that grease. The grease is your money, and money is good. Maybe you're an artist, in the middle of painting a portrait, landscape, or some sort of abstract piece. Well guess what, millions of people are going to want to see this when it is done. And someone will then want to own this piece hence purchasing it from you, if they have the ability to know it's there, and that your skills exist.

One important factor when it comes to marketing is loans. A lot of businesses rely on loans. Some struggle to repay them and some even have difficulty just getting one. Some businesses fail, simply because they don't have the money to acquire customers; i.e. advertise. AEY MARKETING helps you overcome all of these obstacles. By bringing customers directly to you, you will have much more revenue streaming in. When you get to a point where you have things on back order, that now means you have more money coming in, even before you can get the order together. What does this mean? This means you don't need loans because you now have the money available from the customers. The customers are lined up with the funds to help you stay ahead and not come out of pocket to produce more inventory. For instance, if I have a skateboard company and I need to increase inventory because I'm expecting a high number of sales, that money will then come out of pocket. If I have 20,000 pending orders because I have more customers than I do product readily available, well guess what? I now have the money I need to purchase all the inventory needed without going to negative in the books. I'd much rather have too many customers than a warehouse full of inventory that I cannot move. Less clients, bad. Too many customers, good!

No matter the type of business you have or may want, whether you are a public figure or a silent partner, no matter what, your business or businesses are affected by people and only people. Without the public you have no business doing anything. No product to sell and most certainly, no service to provide. The world, the economy, and your bills revolve around you having people in your life one way or another. So, if you have some way to bring in an income, and by some glorious miracle it doesn't involve a single other person, in any way, shape, or form, moving money from one place to another, then please let me know. Until that happens, the only way money moves and is made, is by going from one person to another in some fashion or another. One account to another, one pocket to another, and from one hand to another, either by card, cash or some other form of currency. And as long as that continues to happen it's going to involve people. And marketing is the only way to attract business.

A guy with nice abs in an underwear commercial or a girl in a bikini for whatever reason, even if it has absolutely nothing to do with the product that is being sold, is marketing. People attract other people. Models are the greatest form of marketing there is in society. I want to advertise my product, so businesses opt to hire a public figure with a huge following. When we see someone doing or using something, it's easier to envision ourselves being that person doing the same thing. When I sign on to work with a business, I am basically an invisible model and I am everywhere that you want your business and product to be seen. There's no need for me to tell your customers who I am, because I am now just a fishing lure. I'm placed in front of them and I move out of the way as soon as they arrive, so the only thing left to see is your product and your business, or even you!

Chapter 38

Every so often the world is hit by a major disaster. A natural, or even a health disaster. The truth of the matter is this, a disaster of any magnitude impacts the world on some level. Remember COVID? Of course, you do. You might even still have one of those masks in a nearby drawer. That impacted the entire world all at once. It did not discriminate. It destroyed lives, communities, economies, and businesses alike. No matter what happened during this disaster, people still helped one another. We figured out a way to keep life going. How to maintain interaction, keep businesses open, and even adapted in ways to increase sales by being inventive and even creative at times.

We as humans still have a natural wild instinct, no matter what. It doesn't matter who you are, where you live, or even how you grew up. We all have it. It's the same thing any wild animal has. Fight or flight. You can attempt to domesticate a tiger all you want, but guess what? When it's cornered, a natural instinct kicks in to make him fight or run. And I'm no tiger scientist, but if you corner a tiger and piss him off, I'm guessing 9 times out of 10, he will just eat you. This is exactly how we operate as people when we are backed into a corner. We have that same option. Give up or fight back. In this case, we fight back or we lose everything. Through COVID, as well as other disastrous situations we have faced, we fought back. 2020 was an incredibly tough year for most everyone and everything. The entire world was forced to change all at once. Some businesses unfortunately did close while others thrived like never before. When you have absolutely no other option than to take a step back and examine your situation, in dire need, through a microscope, you sometimes see things you may have never seen before. You get ideas you may have not have had, and you may even get motivated like never before. It's sort of a rush of adrenaline coursing through your veins that shoots to your brain and says "I got this. I'm going to succeed no matter what it takes and nothing can stop me."

As you re-examine your business, its needs, your needs, your customer's needs, as well as your employee's needs, you begin to make notes. You jot down what needs to happen ASAP. Picture an EMT approaching a traffic accident. They must assess the situation immediately due to the seriousness of the event. It's life and death for them, and for you, it could very well mean the same thing for your business. What do you do? Where do you start? Either way, you better come up with something pretty damn quick. Do you need to have a massive flash sale to bring in a lot of customers and money immediately? Do you need to adjust operations to adhere to life's current circumstances? Do you need to start shifting more to an online presence in order to attract a wider range of customer? Even the rules and policies have changed due to current state and federal regulations, which is affecting everyone's business worldwide. Suddenly everything, everywhere needs to be handled in a very specified way. How can you still make customers feel comfortable to shop and use your services through panic and hysteria? Easy. By showing others that you are still doing better than ever. Marketing is the one thing besides cockroaches that seem to survive and carry on through virtually anything. You can't stop it. You always need it. In fact, you require it to survive.

"Without marketing, there is nothing."

Marketing precedes all that has ever been known. From the moment man invented fire, marketing was born. Is it ever talked about in history books? Of course. The books themselves, the stories in them along with everything you have ever heard. It's all marketing. The pyramids, Stonehenge, the Grand Canyon, the Great Wall of China. What do you think these are all forms of? 100% marketing. For the exact purpose of everyone to see it. Everything you have ever read about history is complete marketing. Every outfit, piece of armor that was customized, to magnificent castles. All marketing. When your entire life revolves around one major factor, that many don't realize, it becomes an, "Aha!" moment, when pointed out. On a personal note, I'd even go as far as to say that marketing may have been the first thing ever, before anyone even realized what it was.

We've made it through the most devastating times man has ever seen and known. Yet, we manage to pull through and do better than we did before. It's almost as if set-backs make us better, stronger than yesterday. If that's the way it works, then please, throw a disaster my way more frequently so I can become the best that has ever done this. AEY MARKETING is the product of a disaster. My life's hard learned lessons, trials and tribulations, and the detrimental hand that was dealt to all of us during 2020, is what created AEY MARKETING. And it wasn't to benefit me one bit. It was a design based on the rest of the world. I saw something that I wish I could've seen years ago, but it took me being in prison to realize what I was truly capable of, and it's that I can help millions of people. The goal for AEY MARKETING is to help as many people as possible. Before, I was so focused on myself because I came from absolutely nothing. What I never realized, is I was on a path to helping others achieve greatness and financial success with every bit of knowledge I'd accumulated along the way. Those moments of frustration you have aren't there to discourage you from accomplishing things. They are there because whatever it is you are working on should be the very best it can be. The frustration is to ensure quality in what you do, as long as you don't give up and settle for what you have. Think about this for a second. Michael Jordan went from athletically one of the worst players growing up, to becoming the best that's ever done it. Getting cut from college teams didn't discourage him. It told him he needed to really show what he was made of and not what he thought he was. There's a difference.

You might do something and only be satisfied with it because others are satisfied, so you end it there. No. Don't do this. You go until it's the best it can possibly be. If you know for a second it can be done better, made better, or a service can be stepped up for your clients, then do it. Don't sit back and say, "Ah, that's good enough." That half ass attitude will only get you half ass results which will result in your business looking like a half ass company that only half-ass cares, which soon will close because your customers will go to someone doing it bigger and better.

Did you manage to find something on your list of business ideas that we discussed previously, that really grabs you? Good. Now take a moment to write down exactly how you would run it if it was in full operation today. Pretend you are the customer, and write down what you'd expect from this company. When you put yourself in your customers shoes, you will see what they see. And if you don't see what it is you're expecting from this business, then fix it so that you do. If your customer is not happy, then you won't be either. However, don't try and please every single person. Remember, several people will not like you, your business, or your products. And that's totally fine. That's actually normal. What you need to do is ensure that the customers who do come to you are happy. Cater to the group your business is designed for. Once you hone in on this, you will begin to learn, identify, and understand who your target audience is, and what they need or want from you. And as long as they continually want something from you, give it to 'em! I give it to as many people as I can, as hard as possible. And yes, I did realize how that just sounded. But you know what, as I always say to everyone I work with, "Go hard, or go home."

Chapter 39

I branched one of the fastest growing defense companies in the country, into avenues no one thought possible. No one does this. I did. I took something not even meant for the general public and got them to love it, support it, and buy damn near anything I put my logo on. By the time I was done, there were people who didn't even like defense companies who were buying all of our merchandise, just because of what our creed was. How I operated, and how I showed each and every single one of my customers, potential customers, and clients how important they are to myself and my brand. Regardless of what you do, if you work hard and people see you working hard, you will always be appreciated. It's a fact. When have you ever heard someone put someone down due to how hard they work? Never. We have been taught since an early age that hard work is appreciated. All hard work. Plus, hard work leads to self-appreciation.

I understand that I can't just tell you to do something and expect for you to get it done. Otherwise, everyone on the planet would be amazing and successful. Clearly, that's false and an unrealistic outlook to have. However, I in fact operate that way. Ever since I was young, getting things done was just a part of who I was. No question about it. I just figured things out. And often times the outcome was better than anticipated. But what I have asked you to do throughout this entire book so far, is incredibly feasible. It is practical and no, it will not take a miracle. However, if you follow, and do the very few simple tasks, they will greatly benefit and change your life more than you know. And when you ask yourself, "How does this guy know so much about marketing?", remember this. The same exact way a brain surgeon, a scientist, even a professor does their job. Years and years of extensive research, training, and application.

I have tried every possible way. I have found all the errors, the things that work, don't work, may work (depending on your type of business), and even learned how to make things work that most say don't, or wont. I'm a Marine. I adapt and overcome. You're human. You have the ability to do the same exact thing. For me, it's just way more intense. I approach every single deal, business, or scenario like it's a battle field. There's always an enemy somewhere. How do I advance on the enemy and overtake, in this case, succeed? I manage to do it every single time. I come. I see. I conquer. This is the type of mentality you need in your business. The ox pulls the plow. He doesn't plant the seeds, water the crops, or even reap what has been sewn. His main objective is to drive forward with pure power and determination, ensuring that the important stuff gets done. The plow needs the ox, but the ox doesn't need the plow. The ox could care less if he is pulling a plow or not. But when he is pulling that plow, some seriously amazing shit happens. The earth shifts, lives begin to change, simply because he is using his power. By attracting what he naturally does to someone who can benefit from it, they benefit mutually. I'm going with you in the direction that you want to go. I make those deep grooves to drive in those customers and clients that you both want and need.

Tell me this. Would you rather have fliers made, pay someone to drop them off who only cares about being paid to drop fliers off, or would you rather spend the exact same amount if not less, to have someone walk willingly into your business who cares about what you do? I would want the person who is on my team the entire way. Don't worry, I won't be doing all the work alone. During the process of AEY MARKETING hand in hand with you, you will actually learn some marketing tips along the way. The goal, is that my motivation will lead you to expanding your business in ways that make you happy and successful. My first priority is to save you money, and then make you even more.

At one point, I got a little too motivating. I actually had someone tell me they wanted to quit their business to become a marketing representative for AEY. I was flattered, but I couldn't let them stop chasing their dream just to help me with mine. Although he was a go getter, and would have fit in perfectly, it just wasn't his dream. My team is amazing, and yes, we are always working with people all over the world.

If you are looking into a marketing career, there's no one better informed to work with than myself. You will learn things that no book or class could ever teach you, simply because they just don't know. And with AEY, I structured it to pay my reps for how hard they work. Marketing is through and through with me. You have a question; I'll help you with the answer. Want me to take a look at what you're doing? Sure, no problem. I guarantee you that no one will take the time or consideration the way I do in order to assure your business is marketed the way it should be.

When I got out of Federal Prison, I began AEY MARKETING officially in the downstairs den of a friend's house. I set aside an allotted time each day to work on this book between marketing projects. As I went day to day on this, I began to think about everything I'd ever done that led me to this very desk I am sitting at. And believe it or not, it actually crossed my mind to not do this book. People always told me, keep what you do under wraps. Think about yourself first and then consider whether or not you want to help others get to where you are. Well, had I listened to everyone else every time someone gave me advice, I would be a lot further behind in life. It's true. I do what most don't, hence why there's only one of me. Just like you. I attended seminars, listened to speeches, and even workshops just to see what others were talking about. I wanted to see if what others were telling me was accurate. You ever do something that doesn't feel quite right? Going to all of that, felt a bit like that. It felt like a cult. Like I was about to join something I really didn't want to be a part of. It just wasn't for me and had absolutely no value whatsoever to actually helping anyone. People just thought it did.

I had been asked what it is I do at all those events. Whenever I would respond that I was a marketing guru, people would attempt to tell me information that was inaccurate, and wouldn't help a blind monkey in a banana field. And yes, I realize bananas don't grow in fields. And when I asked what they actually did for a living, they would often respond with things like, "I'm a public speaker, motivational speaker, and influencer." Crazy. How can you be those things when you have no clue what it is you're talking about? Why on earth would anyone take tips from someone who doesn't know their elbow from their asshole? But hey, this is the world we live in. When you work for me, it's clear, it makes sense, and the proof that I know what I am talking about is there in front of you. I tell everyone who works with me the same thing. "You can make at least $60,000-$100,000 your first year." The choice is always theirs to make. When's the last time a job told you that? And that doesn't include your annual bonus. We work hard. We help others and I take care of everyone whom I work with. Marketing isn't just sales. It's being there. It's helping people in all aspects of life. It's loving, it's caring, and truly ensuring that those, have exactly what it is that they need.

What I deliver to myself, I deliver to you as well. It's simply having a deeper understanding. And no, I am not going to write a relationship book, but marketing is a certain type of relationship. The better you are at it, the more it will flourish. And the more it flourishes, the more you flourish. However, with marketing, if in fact done my way, the right way, you will get way more back than what you put out. Breaking even is not the goal here. Neither is showing a loss at tax time. When you are in marketing, you are in it to maximize and capitalize. When someone says, "You can only wring so much out of a sponge." I say, "Yeah, you're right." But then I grab another sponge. If you want to be on this side of the fence, then I will teach you, you'll be very successful, and pretty damn happy with what you do. By the way, no marketing degree, college degree, or any specialty degree is required to apply. I want social skills. It's nice that you have a fancy plaque that reminds you of what school you went to, in case you forget, but here we need more than that. What is required is a positive attitude and someone who refuses to be limited. Oh, and creativity doesn't hurt.

I've seen people cry at their jobs before, bosses yelling at them, treated poorly and unfairly. That's also marketing. That tells every single person who saw that, "I do not want to work for this business, or be anywhere near it." Whenever I have accomplished something, I have always stopped and said to myself, "Hell yeah, I'd work for this company." If you hate what you do, and definitely have no interest in wanting to own or run your own business, then give me a call. I'll hire you.

Chapter 40

Some odd things have happened in recent times to myself. By this, I mean throughout the course of me writing this book. More specifically yesterday. After I was sent to Federal Prison, everything that I lost, and that were taken from me by the Feds, I pretty much sucked it up and was finally able to accept it as a loss. Material things can always be replaced, but what's inside of you can never be.

I had bent over backwards to create and make my brand as big as I could. Granted, the primary point of the brand was defense products for the U.S. Government. The public loved it and wanted to be a part of it. So that's when I created and launched all the retail merchandise that was attached to the brand. Being in Federal Prison made me realize it was now time to move on to something bigger and better. I had literally written off everything as a loss. And I shit you not, about 30 seconds after I came to grips with it in my mind, someone approached me and asked to see pictures of the merchandise we had created. So, I showed them. And they love it. The idea behind it, what it stood for, but mainly the revenue it brought in. Believe it or not, a lot of people used to ask me if I missed doing this, and if I had the opportunity, would I ever go back to doing what I did, even if all I could do was the merchandise side of things. I always told them no. And yesterday that changed. Someone approached me and asked me the same question. However, this time he didn't just leave me at my response and walk away. He asked me, "What if I re-launch your brand, fund all the orders, add you on as a partner, and your sole responsibility would be just the marketing side?"

It definitely made me stop for a moment and think. No one had ever approached me with this. He sounded serious. Then he said, "You'll have the choice of a royalty deal from every single product made, or a larger percentage of the entire business without any risk." Meaning I would not be responsible for putting up any monies, and was not responsible for any debt or loss should anything happen. I assure you that it's not every day that this sort of thing happens. You know one person who does this a lot though? Warren Buffet. He buys businesses at lows and relaunches them and makes a killing. In this offer, I wasn't selling. I was keeping a portion and stood to make a very nice chunk of change from it. Plus, this company will be a major client for my new marketing company AEY. It would be a win win in my book. Both figuratively and literally.

When you do things in life that are recognized by many as something positive, people will always remember. Hey, we always remember the good times. In most cases, when someone ends up in Federal Prison, it's hardly ever a good thing. But in my case, it turned out to be one of the greatest things to ever happen in my life. I'm not here for drugs, money laundering, or even anything violent or destructive to my community or my country. I'm here because I was a little too good at something and it really pissed someone else off. But I am over it. So over it. It's done and it's behind me.

For some, meeting an international arms dealer is kind of cool. So, I just smile and bask in the moment when that happens. Shake some hands, take some pictures, and even answer some questions that I can legally answer without getting anyone in trouble. Trust me, I have already been warned several times by the government that if I say certain things, there's a very good chance that I could "disappear" for good.

So, all of this intrigue, dedication, and hard work, led to a major business owner seeing what I was capable of, and requested a sit down, which then led to this offer. And most everyone said I should avoid anything to do with the brand due to it nearly getting me into some serious trouble. I mean Federal Prison is prison. But for me serious trouble would not have been a few years behind bars, it would've been the initial 60 years they were graciously offering me. However, if I were to move forward with this offer, I'm no longer in charge of the company and there are no more defense products involved. The Feds, I'm somewhat positive, would no longer care. I'd be more a consultant, minority owner and the only thing I am responsible for is marketing, which everyone knows is my specialty. With no reference to defense products, no pictures of any firearms or anything that would lead anyone to believe that this new company is involved in anything that it shouldn't be in, should be totally fine. So, I'm not worried. So again, I'm going from nothing back to the top immediately. I can't fail. A few pages back I mentioned, setbacks cause us to get better at what we do. Deep inside, my sole reason in life is to succeed.

"Do better today than you did yesterday, and make tomorrow a better today."

When you get that fire lit, and the right amount of oxygen is introduced, nothing can extinguish it. I thought I had lost my passion for a while, sitting in Federal Prison, but I was nowhere close to losing my drive. It was just a fleeting moment. A very long moment, to sit, regroup, and rethink what I needed to do in order to move forward again. And believe me, this happens all the time to the biggest businesses on the planet. They think they've hit a wall, so they gather their team, have a several meetings to refocus and restructure what will now be their pivot point. Having a pivotal point is needed at times. In fact, it's not only needed, it's necessary. In basketball, if you have no more room to pivot, you either take your shot or take a chance and lose the ball to the opposing team. By having a pivot point, or several, you can now maneuver around your defender (competition, other businesses, obstacles, etc.) to score.

Had I not been instilled with this natural drive, I wouldn't be where I'm at. There's no way I'd be able to construct what I've done in order to help others. When I got out of prison, I expected nothing. To have absolutely nothing and no one. To start completely from scratch all over again. But I couldn't give up, and I didn't.

The day I was released from Federal Prison, like in the movies, where the inmate is released, the guards say "bye", and the big chain link fence closes behind him as he slowly approaches what seemingly is the only vehicle waiting to pick him up, was amazing! However, none of that shit happened. Apparently, that's not a thing. But it was so much better than that. Having a ride was great. There's no exact way to describe the feeling of seeing someone you actually know after not seeing anyone you know for years. And it's not what you think. There were no visits. This was during COVID. We barely had movement on the yard as it was. So, for sure no one was coming to visit. No tablets, no nothing.

Not only was I out, but I was nearly two states over from where I need to be. I had limited time to drive back to the halfway house. A few years of not having any kind of physical contact with anyone that I knew, was tough. And even that didn't get me down. Remember, my mom raised me to be one tough S.O.B. I used every bit of drive I could muster to buckle down and focus. Although I still had several limitations looming over me due to the federal government, I made things happen. When you want something bad enough, you'll find a way to get anything you want and need, accomplished.

Chapter 41

A blessing in disguise is what some would say. I call it, "The hustle that never dies." In doing so, back to my brand. I had my attorney look over the deal for this new offer. I spent some time consulting on new designs, merchandise, and marketing plans. AEY MARKETING would solely be responsible for heavy customer acquisition at virtually pennies on the dollar, due to my formula. As a part owner of any company that I work with, I ensure our customer cost is lower than anyone else can possibly get it for. Hence why I'm kind of a big deal. The real estate mogul that approached me regarding the re-launch of my brand, also hired my company AEY to acquire customers for several other businesses that he owned.

Word spread like wildfire yet again due to my strong work ethic. And my client roster began to grow exponentially. Of course, it didn't hurt that my foundation was the list of celebrities and pro-athletes that I had previously worked for, but my strong work habits, drive, and determination were what struck a chord with everyone. If you end up being lucky enough to work for me, I guarantee your drive, motivation, and damn near everything else in your life will elevate. Except your stress. That will significantly drop.

I could say I'm blessed. I could even say I'm lucky, but I not only promise you, I guarantee you that neither one of those two things had anything to do with it. Being stubborn and never ever taking no for an answer is what got me where I am today.

Most people have this strange fantasy that everything will just work out with the right person. And not only is that a fairytale, but it's complete bullshit. If it seems too good to be true, then it is. You have to work constantly on any relationship, just like a business. Why? Because the harder you work, the better it gets. And trust me, being in that situation, life is never boring.

Marketing is all about putting yourself out there, on every level. If you're shy, that's fine. Partner up with a super fun loudmouth who gets attention everywhere they go. Be seen. Be heard. Make a spectacle if you must. You know the vendors at the sporting events who are constantly screaming their faces off? "Get your peanuts and ice-cold beer!" If they don't yell and look crazy, you'd never get your snacks and you most certainly wouldn't know they just passed you by. Grab your snacks, grab your beers, and don't let these opportunities pass you by. And if you're the vendor, and I see you out there in public, I might just make an ass of myself to help you out. That aisle you walk up and down, all those stairs between the seats in that massive stadium, is literally a money trail. Your sole purpose is to walk that path and collect money. You don't even need to ask for it. People are practically breaking their necks, tripping over one another to get their hard-earned money to you. Hell, some people even get frustrated when the vendor isn't nearby. Which in this case, causes some to yell just as loud as the vendors.

People want what you have, and you want what the people have. It's an even exchange. When you grasp your customer's and client's attention, engage. You now have developed the opportunity for return clients. Something that every business on the planet strives for. Getting them to buy is one thing. Getting them to come back is entirely another. There are tons of businesses who get my repeated business and yours as well. In fact, during NASCAR season, there's one major Brazilian owned company that forever will keep me as a customer. Anheuser-Busch. Bud-Light is my NASCAR beer of choice. And when I'm balls deep in a Talladega or Daytona race, I plow through cases with friends and family like I'm a tractor. It's just my thing. Just like you have your thing. In fact, what is your thing? What company has done so well or keeps doing so well that you love it so much? Why do you keep going back to them? These are the key questions you can ask yourself. These answers are what makes these companies successful. My brand is the same thing. Investors approach me because they love it. Every person who has ever said something positive about my brand, customer or investor has purchased from me multiple times. I've often had new customers on the spot turn around and immediately ask how they can invest in my company. That's how you know you're doing something right. When your customer wants more from you than just something to buy.

Chapter 42

Passion is where it starts. It's one thing to have a good idea or a product, and completely another to have passion behind it. When you talk about it, do people get excited based on your passion alone? Your eyes should be lighting up. And when you explain this product or idea to someone, it better seem like you've just discovered the cure for cancer. Like it's the greatest thing on earth. Sometimes, this happens by mistake. I'll get a question, and before I know it, I'm five minutes into the most excited response this person has ever heard before I catch myself.

Just for someone to say, "Wow, you really are passionate about this, please tell me more?" is a huge deal. Remember, marketing is all about delivery. Who cares that Domino's pizza has had the same exact tasting pizza for the last 100 years or so. Suddenly they now have driverless vehicles bringing your pizza to your home. How cool is that? You've now focused on the method they use rather than their product itself. Marketing! Clearly the pizza didn't get any better, but you don't care.

I was recently at a pool party in Las Vegas, Nevada. It was at a really nice casino. What I saw completely blew my mind. And it's not what you think. The pool got a smart delivery idea. Their new marketing method was what made it amazing. A bottle of champagne is readily available to order from almost any cocktail server. A bottle you can purchase yourself at a local store for about $100, was now $500 if someone brought it to you. That same bottle is now $2,500. How? and why? Well, we all love attention. So, when the pool found a way to make every single person stop what they were doing to look at this bottle of champagne flying your way, they nailed it. Your bottle is now being delivered to you via drone. A fucking drone is flying your bottle of $100 shit, to you, and it jumped nearly $2,400 in value for this. Why? Just so everyone can see how damn cool this is, and then, who is it that's doing this? It attracts attention like no other. So as a business, this $100 bottle which they get wholesale for closer to $45, has now grossed nearly $2,455 for just a couple minutes of work. Well, that drone investment cleared up real fast. And nearly the cost of the next case of bottles are covered. Now that's what I call genius marketing.

They created a wow factor and are making a killing at it. Everyone sees this and now they all want that VIP experience. And guess what, they are more than willing to pay for it just to look cool. You know what this tells me? That even if you want to own your own business, maybe you don't have a service, or product you created, you can still purchase stuff wholesale like most other people, and just make the delivery unique. Your approach is everything. People are approached all the time with products they don't buy. But the one time they do, when it finally happens, it's not because they broke down and gave in, but it's all in how they were approached.

When you go to Benihana's, it's not because you enjoy eating flaming onions directly off a stove, hell you can get a flaming onion pretty much at Burger King, it's because their delivery. The chef who cooks your food right in front of you. He interacts with you, makes jokes, flips the food around, does a cool trick with an egg (don't know why), flings the food as if it's some Harlem Globetrotter game right into your mouth from clear across the grill. It's a show. You can get dinner anywhere, but if you want it to be exciting, then Benihana's is where you go. So, take your inquisition to a different area. Think outside the box. Find something people use every day, and get creative with your delivery. Re-brand it, put your logo on it, and make it more fun or convenient than it appears to be.

A nightclub gets away with selling a bottle of $185 Cristal Champagne for $1,500 because you get to sit in a comfortable booth with your friends, enjoy music, and the fun that surrounds it. Sure, you could go to Costco or Sam's Club and just buy the bottle for $185, which seems like a much better deal. But what are you going to do? Sit in the parking lot and drink it? Go home and drink it alone in your living room? Where's the fun in that? The experience is everything. You're not just marketing a product, a service, or your business. You're marketing the experience that goes along with it.

If your passion is movies, maybe you get into a surround sound installation company. This way you can deliver the full experience of how the film should sound. To feel something, is why we do everything. Why else do you spend thousands of dollars and wait in the blistering hot sun at Disneyland? Not for yourself. It's so your children can have that magical experience. Disney understands your pain and now that's why they sell beer at Disneyland. Now you and your children can enjoy the experience. Trust me, Mickey Mouse is way more fun when you're shitfaced. Just don't tell your kids that. Make what you do, or have, worth someone's while. If you can do this, and truly display enthusiasm, you're winning!

As I market more, I begin to find a lot more businesses who are doing great. Part of my passion is finding those who love what they do, and are exceptional at it. When I watch shows like ABC's Shark Tank, most of their primary concerns involve marketing. If you don't have a great marketing infrastructure in place, they're not even interested in whatever you may have. It pains me to see those who are spending $30 - $100 on customer acquisition. I see these companies and definitely get the urge to reach out to them to offer a partnership with AEY MARKETING. Although that's not what our primary objective was, it has begun to shift more into that area. Chances are, you don't need the shark or the loan if you have great marketing.

It's like the old catch twenty-two that happens to many when applying for their first waitressing job. They are often told, "You need waitressing experience to work here." But how do you get that experience, when you don't have it, and need it for the job that's looking for it? The chicken or the egg? But now with what I have done, none of that is even relevant. I skipped right over all of it, making it completely unnecessary. With the AEY MARKETING formula, you don't need experience. Even if your business has no marketing infrastructure, I've single handedly proven it doesn't matter. If your business is established or even just starting, that's my specialty, bringing your brand-new customer base to you. The solution that many businesses rely on, never existed really until now. The problem will always be customer acquisition, and my formula proves it can be done with absolutely zero knowledge on your part. Get your passion on and find something fun and exciting that makes you appreciate life. Because I guarantee you that if there is something you truly love, or love doing, then there is an entire group of people out there somewhere who feel the exact same way.

My passion clearly is marketing. My book is so thoroughly about marketing that I even plugged several businesses in this book. You're welcome. I could've easily said a place and described it as "so and so", or a typical business that does "these types of things", but I didn't. I mentioned them by name. By simply mentioning these businesses in this book about marketing, I've just now indirectly advertised and potentially made more sales for them. How many? Who knows? Who cares? But what does matter is that I am the best to ever do this, yet I still go out of my way to freely market other businesses. Whether it's by reference or personal experience, clearly, they are mentioned because they are doing something right. Not everyone will agree with me, but according to myself, and more importantly the accountants who work for some of these companies, they'll tell you they are definitely doing something right.

Money doesn't lie. And if you have a shitload of it, then I can assure you your marketing is well on point. I learned from the best, and strived to be better. I am truly a master at social media marketing. AEY MARKETING, can handle any business out there, anywhere in the world. If the U.S. Government would let me market the moon (because apparently, we own it?), I would market the hell out of it. The moons social media page would have millions of followers and before you know it, people would be purchasing plots and investing in more projects in space. (Footnote, people have already begun to buy plots on the moon.) Think I'm joking? For fun, I just texted a buddy of mine and said, "The government just put me in charge of selling home plots on a specific spot on the moon." Without question he responded, "How big are the available plots, and how much?" See! Even me. I'd buy anything you have if you marketed it properly.

One day, I bought two different Mercedes, an SL55 and a SUV, the ML55 AMG, a new motorcycle, a new Denali, and a mega cab turbo Cummins diesel Dodge Ram. Yes, all in one day. Did I really need five fucking vehicles? Absolutely not. But I was sold! And on that particular day, I was really only looking for a motorcycle. Somehow, by the end of the day, I had a new motorcycle, and 4 brand new vehicles delivered to my house. I've toned things down since then. I had a nice lifted truck, a decent muscle car and a couple of motorcycles. Again, all because of marketing.

Chapter 43

With reproach and this new deal to relaunch my defense brand (just the merchandise side), we began to expand into the sports world. Surfboards, skateboards, snowboards, hell, even maybe fence boards. Just kidding. Someone will always be there to say, "Hey, you're doing too much", and I'll always be there to remind them that they are not doing nearly enough.

I'm working on a new liquor brand. I can't even tell you how much time I have already put into it. Also began discussing a scotch line and vodka. This idea has been one that's floated around in my mind for quite some time. It took some discussion, and with the right things in place, moving forward with it would be an ideal investment. What is one of your ideas that's been floating around? I know for years, that you've had an idea that you thought would be cool to get into. Maybe it's time you did. If you're ready, then so am I. Let's do this together.

A business owner once told me, "I don't wish to expand, because if I do, I feel that my customers won't get my personal touch and service if I'm not personally there." And I think that is a perfectly logical response to have. I honestly can't argue with that. As a matter of fact, most people feel that way or have at some point while running their business. But here's where we expand on that. You can maintain that exceptional touch, and service, throughout your entire business, even if it's a location that is clear across the country. How can you ensure quality service and touch without being somewhere? By setting an example.

Setting rules and guidelines for your employees to follow. Standards are a huge thing and the main reason why franchises and multiple locations do so well. All employees must adhere to your strict rules and guidelines that you have set forth in order to operate at a certain level. This way, everything flows smoothly. If you can get this down, no matter the location, no matter who is working there, each and every customer and client will feel like the person helping them is a personal acquaintance of yours. That personal touch and service will come from them as if it's an extension of you. So physically you may not be there, but your products, quality, and customer service will be that as if you were. And that's exactly what you want. Marketing that personal touch is a key factor to the reason so many businesses thrive.

When I explained this to a particular business owner, at first, she was hesitant. And by the end of the conversation, she both understood and agreed that this made sense and that it works. She had been so used to being hands on that she never had the chance to step back and be that fulltime owner. Many people do this and end up becoming their own employee. It's good to know how to operate your business, as it will give you a firsthand look at day-to-day operations (i.e. what needs to be done and what's missing). This is perfect as it will give you the chance to see what your customers see, as well as what they don't see. And being on the ground level is key for marketing. A customer or client may ask you a question that either needs to be answered a specific way, or it may even be possible that you don't know the answer altogether, which in itself is a good learning experience. This is the type of information that you will pass on to your employees so your operation continues to flow smoothly.

After discussing all of this with the same business owner that I had mentioned, we began to discuss marketing strategies. She believed that the only way someone could know how good her business was, was to simply come in and experience it for one's self. This is true, in one aspect. If you are coming in to the business, you are able to experience the environment, the employees, and possibly the food and drinks if that's the type of establishment you have (which in this case it is). "What about the other way?" She looked at me blankly. She said, "What do you mean the other way? What other way is there? How can someone experience your business part of your business without physically being there? And why does that matter?" She asked all the right questions without even realizing it. In today's society, the moment someone enters an establishment, nearly 99.9% of the time, their cell phone is in their hand or nearby. Which means, they are going to post a review, a comment, or even a suggestion regarding your business. And who sees this? Everyone. People who have been there, people who haven't been there, and now potentially people who may never come there or return due to some of the reviews.

This I explained to her, like other business owners, is the "outer body" experience of a business. This is engaging in part, and a very effective avenue of a business without physically being there. This is something that is common worldwide. If someone reads reviews about your business, and has never been there, this is taken into consideration if that person will even visit your establishment. I've seen reviews sink a business. Now, this business owner that I had been speaking with, she was coming around to seeing the outside experience of her business, the way to experience it so to speak without physically being there. She admitted that she had not ever considered this. So, I volunteered some time to personally help her out. Needless to say, she gets it. She has opened a second location on the other side of town already. She floats back and forth from one location to another and is slowly learning to be an owner versus owner-employee.

Sometimes people feel if they let go and step back, that things will automatically crumble. And they will, if your business foundation is built on a popsicle stick design. It can only withstand so much before it has no choice but to collapse. Structure is also marketing. You are marketing to your staff, future employees, as well as customers and clients, saying that your business is stable. It's trustworthy and anyone who is a part of it in any way has absolutely nothing to worry about. Safety and security are everything in your business. It's so important that there are businesses who solely market items such as safety and security. ADT, Brinks, and other home security companies are perfect examples of this. Their marketing key is not just the systems they sell, but the signs and stickers that are placed on your property. It does two things. It tells the public you have an alarm, so they hopefully don't break into your shit, and two, it lets other people know what company is doing the "protecting." Marketing is limitless. I have built a global social media marketing company that is also limitless. So, expand, franchise, and be that business owner with the proper structure in place. With the appropriate marketing, AEY can ensure that your concerns will be minimal. So next time someone approaches you to start a new business, or expand a current one in a new city, state, country, hell, even on a new planet, just know as long as your marketing is with us, that's half the battle. And we will win those battles every single time.

I get questions regarding marketing nearly seven days a week. It makes some people a bit nervous until I begin speaking with them, then they start to relax a bit. The unknown is always unnerving. People ask, "What should I post? What should I advertise? How do I know if my website will work?" Doesn't matter. Of course, it matters that it's operational and functional, but your primary concern should be customer and client acquisition. You're marketing in order to bring revenue into your business. I've seen some of the worst websites that look like they were constructed by a blind window licker, and the business is thriving. How? Because people don't care what color your website is. They care more about you being upfront, honest, and have something that they want to buy. So go ahead and tell your twenty-something year old pothead IT guy to make it awesome, because he or she will definitely know how to attract the current generation of spenders.

Your job is to own the business and ensure clients and customers are steadily coming in. Worry about what's making you money. I promise you that the border color of your website isn't going to make you any money. It's just going to give you something else that's incredibly unnecessary to worry about. But if it really bothers you that much, then I have absolutely no problem throwing in my two cents if that will help you decide on what color it should be to attract more people. Afterall, advice is what I'm here for.

The biggest question I usually get is, "How?" How is it that I do what it is that I do? I often respond to this with my hands open and out to the sides, palms facing upwards. I shrug and smile. Afterall, the colonel isn't going to tell you the recipe to his special blend of herbs and spices that he uses for his world-famous Kentucky Fried Chicken, is he? Is McDonald's going to tell you how they make their secret sauce? Don't think so. My secret recipe however, does involve something that I will in fact share with you. Hard work. What I do is not easy, but I do what I do amazingly well.

Prior to my prison sentence, part of a daily marketing ploy on my part was too open carry a firearm right there on my hip. Why? Fashion, that's why. It might sound crazy, but check this out. As a defense contractor you are known for your weapons. So why wouldn't I be seen with something I use? It just makes sense to me. I had many different color firearms that I wore depending on the color of my outfit that day. Of course, everyone who saw me would comment. They thought it was crazy how I turned it more into an accessory. But you see what I did there? It sparked conversation everywhere I went, without me having to say anything, which then led those people into being potential customers and purchasing merchandise. Sometimes the craziest shit actually works. I even bought shoes based on the type of firearms I owned. Again. Why? Because different firearms are made for different uses, and having the proper attire, especially on your feet, determines better maneuverability while in motion.

Look at Kim Kardashian. One homemade porn launches her career to heights that both her and Ray J could have never imagined. The guy has his own wireless ear buds, television show, and more. And we all know what Kim has. Everything. She as marketed so well that nine times out of ten you say just the word Kim and most people know which Kim you are talking about.

Chapter 44

Marketing is a functional asset. And being able to function properly is everything. And this is exactly where the science of marketing comes into play. The microscopic portions of it that are more than most skimmed right over. Back to an athlete topic really quick. So, athletes go to a class that teaches them how to do that super cool ass sports signature that somehow all athletes can do. They (some of them, depending on the position they may and the type of sport), spend hours working on poses for when they score. Not that it makes them better, but so the public can mimic something their favorite player is doing without having to be an actual athlete. It's like a connection. Having stats is great and gets you paid. Having a cool "signature move" helps gets you memorable endorsement deals. Marketing! People love symbols, images, and things that have meaning. People even get tattoos apparently to remind them to do certain things or be a certain way, as if they'll forget. "Stay True", "Stop Snitchin", or "Don't forget to pick the kids up from school." I think that last one may not be a real tattoo, but I bet someone's going to get it now.

When people ask me, "What should I market?" or "Which part of my business should I really put out there?" I tell them, put the "YOU" part out there. The part that represents you and who your business really is. If you are still not sure exactly what part that may be, then go with what your favorite part of your business is. When you are marketing, always be thinking about what the customer wants, not the owner. The owner wants to get paid, and in order to do so, the customers need to see exactly why they should give you, their money.

I've always had this notion to own and operate a bar, more for fun than anything. But no matter how much I would love to, that dream is shot for me. Pretty much anything involving a license coming from my favorite agency, the ATF, is shot down. They regulate alcohol, tobacco, firearms and now, explosives. My name comes across their desk for any reason whatsoever, especially for a bar license, I can pretty much guarantee you it will go straight in the trash. But let's say I could own a bar. Hell, let's say you are about to, or considering opening a new one, buying an old one and fixing it up. Here's what I would do as an example of marketing. Find all the other bars nearby. See what they offer. Even go to hang out on their busiest night and see how they operate, who they cater to, and get a feel for the area. Now figure out if this is the same crowd you want to appeal to. If it is, great. If not, no worries, this marketing strategy will work wonders for you.

Begin marketing a night that no bar near you is marketing. Do some crazy specials that night, and only on that night. This will begin to draw a crowd. This crowd, well some of them, may begin to come in on the weekends. If you start to see customers coming to your bar from another bar, great! As this will happen. Set up an iPad and get everyone's email address that's coming in. As soon as people ask why, and your response is that it's because you are sending them a digital coupon for free drinks every week that they come in (more than likely a well shot), they won't second guess it. Free alcohol you say? Everyone's signing up at that point. Your first thought is, how does this make me money? Easy! No one is going all the way to a bar just for a single shot. They will purchase a drink every single time, guaranteed. On average, a bar patron purchases at least 3-4 drinks during their visit. Now let's say your bottle of well alcohol is roughly $10, and let's say for this example that you can squeeze about 20 shots out of this particular bottle. Your customer cost is now .50 cents per customer. Now you've just spent .50 cents on one customer to now turn around and receive nearly $15, before tip, from that customer. Let's say they purchase a slightly more expensive drink, now you've had that spend customer $20 with a .50 cent advertisement. Your cheap and very effective marketing strategy has landed you a gross return of $14.50. Not bad huh? And since most people don't go to a bar alone, you've now tripled, maybe quadrupled that number. Each guest that someone has brought, you are now going to get their email, so on their next visit they get the same offer.

Guess what starts to happen here? Everyone who goes to a bar, now takes pictures of themselves and their friends having a good time. The moment someone posts that they have received a free drink from your establishment, you basically now have more customers on the way in to your place of business. There's no need for fliers, billboards, television ads, or anything like that. Social media has done wonders for your local business. But with a bar, that's just the beginning. Have not just karaoke night, but a contest where people can win money, college night, industry night, even let veterans get that sweet little discount for serving their country. Know who else spends a lot of money on booze? Lawyers and cops. Catch my drift? And these types of people always spend a lot, because they drink a lot. Plus, they never come alone. They bring all their friends.

When you're marketing, you have to be creative, and maybe a bit crazy in order to think outside the box. You see how simple these ideas are? They are effective and produce a positive cash flow. No one has ever caught a fish by paddling their boat out to the middle of the lake and expecting the fish to hop right in. Not realistic at all. You've got to throw something out there and reel 'em on in. Or use a spear. But it's not exactly legal to spear people to get them into your establishment. It would be like a car salesman locking you in the vehicle until you purchased it. Being super aggressive, way too much work and it may cost you your income. Don't do it. It's crazy to say but a lot of business owners are against giving things away. But I must clarify one major thing, you're not giving anything away. What you are doing is simply utilizing funds that you are spending on marketing anyways, just in a different area and spending a lot less to get better results. What do you think? Do you think you a have a better chance of getting me into your bar with a flier on my car, or a free drink offer?

Don't know about you, but there's already enough parking lots littered with fliers from who knows what, from who knows where. Also, when you hand someone a flier, it's like saying, "Here, you throw this away for me." But the great thing about advertising on fliers is even if no one calls back, uses your coupons, or simply just picks one up, it's not a total loss. Statistics show that 1%-10% of fliers are in fact picked up, read, and even used. The rest are out there to display your business. It's like a bumper sticker. You'll come across the same one and say, "Hey! I've seen that one before." Recognition. You might get bumper stickers made to advertise your business and then strategically place them on every intersection, on light poles and posts. Not saying this is the best thing to do, for several reasons, but you might do this simply so the general public subliminally remembers your business. Just don't get in trouble for defacing property while doing so. Bands do it, hell, even homeowners do it with something as simple as yard sale signs.

Chapter 45

People ask me, "Why do you need commercials for a marketing company?" Because it works. That's why. Some commercials are for business to consumer, which nearly all of them are for that specific reason. Mine are targeted towards other businesses. Now why would I advertise to other businesses? Because that's my demographic. Most big businesses do not run their own social media pages, however, there are still quite a few of them do in fact with an inhouse team.

Every business owner at some point watches television. And it's at this point they will see things a bit differently than they do throughout their busy day. A business owner is more likely to contact me when their day is over because they don't like to be interrupted during the time they are focused on day-to-day operations. Although AEY heavily impacts every business when it comes to a financial aspect, this is something that takes some serious focus. I need the business owner to be free from any type of distraction so they can focus on the most important part of their company. The money. Without the money, you have no business. So, while you are at home, watching MTV, VH-1, Comedy Central, Fox, ESPN, or whatever channel our commercial may air on, you will for sure notice it. You have now put your day behind you and are in that rare moment to take on literally nothing else but relaxation. So now, when my commercial pops up somewhere, whether you are relaxing, or just checking your social media, you are more inclined to be in a better mood and pay more attention to something that may benefit you.

While most commercials are hoping to catch a few interested buyers, I am not. My primary focus is every single business owner, potential business owner, social media influencer, athlete, musician, artist, and more! My demographic is literally anyone and everyone who utilizes social media for any possible reason to make money. While we have that elite focus, and level of experience, AEY MARKETING has its focus on all types of clients, all over, all the time. AEY will treat you with the same exact courtesy and professionalism as all the celebrities I have personally ever worked with. For several years, I moonlighted as a celebrity bodyguard. The most influential and loved people on the planet entrusted me with their lives. People normally ask me to work with them due to my level of dedication. "You would put your life on the line for someone you don't know?" Of course, I would. I'm a Marine. It's in my DNA. I did it for my country and in my personal life, I have done it for many others. Why? Because someone has to. Believe it or not, some people hire me for marketing based on those few things alone. The fact that I am that damn good at marketing is just a bonus. So, I would like to think that this is the main reason people hire me. But if we package it altogether, then it comes down to dedication and knowledge. The dedication to be the best at what I do, and the knowledge to do so.

Chapter 46

Let's break marketing down really quick. If you want to know what marketing truly is, then here it goes. At its most basic form, marketing comes down to socializing. Seriously up to this point I've given you every angle, every example, and have even told you exactly how this is done. But at its very core, no matter what anyone says, it's socializing. I don't care if you have a Ph.D. in marketing, and your grandfather was involved in marketing, then your father, and now you. End of the day, it's socializing. There are thousands of books on the market, to teach you about marketing, how it's done, and what the best ways to get your business out there are. Truthfully, the best way is the way that works. The way that increases your client base, business awareness, and most important, revenue! If it's not doing all three, then that's fine. If at the end of the day it somehow is increasing your revenue and you see a steady increase in profits, then it's working.

"If you can socialize, you can market."

"What works for some may not always work for others."

These in fact are true statements. It just doesn't apply here at AEY MARKETING. Anyone can learn how to market, but not everyone is good at socializing. Well, exactly what is socializing? Is it being the life of the party? Being able to shake hands, smile and say hello to people? Or is it simply being open, vulnerable, and friendly? It's all of the above. It's any of the above. Here's the thing though. You may be able to read, even study, and a have a great idea of what socializing may in fact be, however, doing it, even for the first time, can be quite nerve racking for some. Some people are just naturals and can light up any room they walk in to. While others are more quiet, mysterious, and deliver the same inquisitive look that the life of the party exhibits.

Whenever you are with your buddies, your girlfriend, or whomever, what is it that you are doing? You are socializing, right? Hanging out, talking about the news, sports, weather, the latest gossip about friends, it's all natural. You are doing it without any real thought. We do this at every point in our lives virtually with everyone we know. We discuss our favorite cars, drinks, restaurants, hobbies, and more. We are constantly telling someone something, that we presume is important, exciting, or intriguing. This is marketing. This is socializing. More commonly referred to professionals in business marketing as "word of mouth" advertising.

This form of advertising is older than any other form of marketing and works wonders. So, the next time you are spending time with a friend, relative, or a loved one, remember this, your socialization skills are what makes the world go round. Your single conversation with another individual has more of an impact than you can possibly imagine. This is very real. A single conversation can affect an entire population of people even halfway around the world. Our government does it all the time. What comes out of that conversation, can then change the way we view some country far away. What we once thought about some nation, has severely flipped due to what two specific people have just discussed.

Socializing leads to change. By socializing, you my friend are on the ground level of marketing. Now, walking up to a complete stranger the way I did as a child, is an entirely different level of socialization. That comes from a place that unfortunately not many will get to experience. Why? Because I come from what might be the last generation of people who didn't grow up having cell phones, texting, or Google, but instead had to actually go outside, into direct sunlight, and interact with another human being to learn something. My socialization skills were bred out of pure survival. Eat or starve. Live or die. Win or lose.

Most of us don't fully understand every single aspect of marketing. And that's fine. It would be damn near impossible for everyone to know everything. However, we all have an understanding of what marketing is used for, and why we use it. Learn what it is you need to know about marketing and leave the rest to those (me), who are professionally mastering this field. Keep in mind, you certainly don't have to understand all of the inner details of marketing to know that your business will benefit greatly from it. Hell, most of us have no clue how a car even works. We just think that we put gas in it, turn the key, start it up, put it in drive, and hit the accelerator. What we do have though, is a basic understanding of how a car will get us from point A to point B. And that's more than enough for most, unless you have the intention of being a mechanic, in which case, if your knowledge does not exceed that, then I suggest you learn as you will see that you soon will have no customers. If my car breaks down, I go to the toolbox, aka the wallet. Because if I'm not out of gas, then there's no way on earth I could even begin to guess what is wrong. Hence why I am not a mechanic and should never ever attempt to work on my own vehicle. But when it comes to marketing, I'm basically the Nobel Peace Prize winner of this. Global social media marketing. This is what I know. This I do, and I do this very well. With what I have personally formulated AEY MARKETING to accomplish. No other form of marketing can even compare. Not a single angle aside from what I do can even begin to deliver the results that AEY can. And it's all because I go deeper than anyone else is willing to go in this field.

By understanding what AEY MARKETING is all about, what we do, and how hard we work to do it, is having a brand-new view on one of the oldest things known to man. I can almost assure you that thousands of years ago, there were no clothing stores to advertise that hot new leather crotch cover, or the internet to look up what other cultures were doing and wearing. None of that existed. It was 100% word of mouth, and to make it even worse, most people didn't even understand what other people were saying, but they still got the message across. It was loud and clear in a way that only us humans could understand. I have gone back that far, to make AEY MARKETING what it is today. Yeah, we might use the latest technology and gadgets that some people have never heard of, or seen, but we do it based on a principle that dates back to the beginning of time.

No two sides of marketing are the same. Each approach is unique for every individual as well as their business. If your business targets mainly international clients, you wouldn't start by renting local billboards in your neighborhood. Your angle then, becomes a way to market to your international clients. If you own a local tire shop, then you would definitely want a strong local presence. That would benefit you the most. If you promote concerts for instance, depending on the type of music that will be playing at an upcoming event, you would start then by advertising on the local station that plays that type of music. And if your business caters to a local elderly crowd, you would then focus more on a daytime local television channel that airs show folks in that age group are prone to watching. You wouldn't market the "Hurry Cane" on Comedy Central or MTV. In the sense that you're targeting a specific group, there are clear, cut, and very legitimate avenues to take regarding this approach. Almost nothing is guaranteed. That being said, each and every one of these options isn't exactly cheap either, and usually requires you to do some depth of research. And of course, you could take one, even several of these options, and see that it still may not work. And again, you could always take your vehicle to the neighborhood mechanic so they can tear your entire vehicle apart without knowing what the primary issue is. If it needs new spark plugs, then why is he tearing the engine block apart? My point exactly.

You go to a reliable mechanic, they plug in the reader and it will give them a basis to start from. This is exactly what AEY MARKETING does. We don't guess. I don't guess. There's no shooting in the dark to try and guess what your customer and client base is or should be. This formulation has been carefully put together so it can be maximized. I've put together a proven method that's guaranteed to work. Unlike specific avenues that are designed to reach a particular demographic, AEY MARKETING does it all. A billboard can't, a magazine advertisement can't, and solely a television commercial damn sure can't.

AEY MARKETING accomplishes what television, fliers, billboards, radio, and magazines do, all in one. Is it better to have AEY MARKETING do what the others can't? Definitely. You get all of that and more out of what I've perfected. A reach unlike any other with measured results, unlike the rest. I'm not saying don't utilize those avenues. I'm simply saying that my method is a thousand times more effective. Yeah, it's great to see your business on a 50ft billboard every time you are out and about, but if it's not helping you increase your revenue, then it's simply wasted marketing dollars. And that can be a lot of marketing dollars going down the drain. Some spend an upwards of $50,000 a month on combined efforts to market their business, while some spend as little as $500 a month. It's not necessarily how much you spend either. It's what you are hoping to accomplish. Hopefully you have or do discuss this with your business partners or review it alone if you are a sole owner.

To market is to have a specific goal in mind. You don't just grab the ball and head any which way up and down the court or field as you please, because if you don't pay attention, you can quickly find yourself doing the exact opposite of what was intended. There is a focal point. Once you see this, you take the ball, and head in that direction as quickly as humanly possible, and you score. And you score again.

Fortunately for myself and AEY MARKETING, we are not limited by human speed. With our technology and strategies, I've implored, you could say I have the ability to move at the speed of sound, maybe almost faster than a speeding bullet. And by being the best to do this, it's not possible to let anyone down. You get results every single time. You have a solid support structure all the time. I won't treat your business like family, the type of family you don't want to be around. No, we treat you and your business as if it's our very own. Because in a way it is. To market your company, our name is going behind you, and we would not want to get into something to look bad. I'm pushing your company, your product, or your service, because I believe in it. I believe in you. During game time, we give it 100%. However, when the game is over, and you go home to relax, recover, and enjoy an exciting and successful day, we are still at the office working on the next day's gameplan for you to succeed yet again. When the next day comes, and you step out into your business arena, we are there with you, backing every play you make.

Our goal is not necessarily to just help you, but to make sure we increase your annual revenue by as much as possible. I've never heard a billboard, magazine, television, or radio advertisement tell me this before. But I am telling you, and letting you know we are hands on the entire way. You want more? I'll give you more, but AEY MARKETING will not give you any less. What does a billboard company do for you once your advertisement is posted up? Nothing. Well, that's not entirely true. At the end of the month, they contact you to pay for the next month. However, in between that time, they are completely hands off. You have the ability to maintain contact with us 24/7. I'm sure you want more out of your business, as we want that for you as well. And unlike any other form of marketing, you are able to track what we do for you daily! Not a soul can tell you exactly how many people saw your magazine ad, heard your radio advertisement, or saw your television commercial. No one can give you those definitive numbers that would help keep you informed of things like trends, or how to gauge your inventory levels. And they sure can't tell you who is quickly becoming interested in what you do, until way after the campaign is over. AEY MARKETING specializes in all of that ahead of time without delay.

By having daily, up to date information, this helps your business in ways that nothing else can. This is what people have been trying to accomplish for years. Staying ahead. Getting ahead and exceeding the previous day's progress. And now you can. AEY MARKETING strategies are for all levels of business. Whether you are just starting out or if you want to grow significantly, we can bring you all the customers and clients that you can handle. You should understand something though, there is an endless amount of people out there who are interested in your business, whatever it may be. Think about this. Every business has to bring in customers from somewhere, right? We just happen to specialize in a particular method that can locate those customers day after day, worldwide. By streamlining these people direct to you, and your business, you have successfully cut out a middle man (i.e. other advertisement ideas), thus saving you a buttload of money.

So, tell me something, do you think it would be beneficial to have customers already lined up to hand their hard-earned money over to you? Or would you rather go out into the middle of the lake, sit for hours each day, utilizing the time you have which is incredibly valuable, to wait and see if any customers randomly pop up and jump right into your big shiny boat? I'm quite sure it's both smarter and less time consuming to do what you need to do, while those customers are being ushered in by the truckloads so to speak. By the way, I don't even like fishing. I'd rather hire someone to get all the fish I need if that's the case. Why? Because I have absolutely no idea what I am doing.

Speaking of not knowing what I am doing in certain situations, I absolutely love learning new things. For instance, one of my all-time favorite things to do is listen to business pitches. This may sound a bit geeky, but I could listen to elevator pitches all day long. However, I enjoy listening to a new business owner tell me about their business, how it works, what they do, why they got into it, and what they hope to accomplish with it. It's the passion behind what people do. It gets me motivated. Pumped! While some people get all jacked up on Mountain Dew, I get that same adrenaline rush from you. When we Skype,

FaceTime, or I swing by your business, please, take your time, and tell me all about it. The more detailed you get the better. Remember, you're not just trying to tell me all this amazing stuff, by doing this, you are socializing and telling me something you believe to be amazing. And by doing so, I get excited! Get me to see what you do. Show me your best product, your service, in the way that I have no idea what it is, but absolutely dying to find out about. Every little detail counts. When you do that, it allows me to harness that same positive energy that you are putting out. And in turn, I deliver that through AEY MARKETING right to your customers.

My absolute favorite is when someone is explaining their business, and as they get more into it, it's as though they have just smashed five Red Bull energy drinks. That's the energy level I am looking for. That's the type of energy AEY MARKETING feeds off of. And that's the same energy that is going to keep your customers coming back again and again. When you are excited, it shows. It's almost infectious in the sense that those near you feel that same excitement and begin to see where you are coming from. Get someone excited about your product or service, and I guarantee you they will be a lifelong user of whatever it is you are selling.

I've had telemarketers call me in the past and nearly put me to sleep on the phone. I'd wait for them to finish their pitch (this is something I would do if I was at home and had time to kill), and right before I would nearly pass out from boredom, my response would be something like, "Are you serious?" For a split second they think they have a sale. Wrong. "Are you serious? You believe that's going to work?", is what I mean. Then normally comes that awkward silence. And for fun I would help them. "Look man. Since you're at work anyways, you might as well put some excitement into it. At least make some money while you are there." And they would give me some bullshit excuse as to how excited can someone get over the phone. So, I would reverse sell them. I asked them the gist of their spiel, and began to flip it on them. "How did you do that?" I explained that people call each other all the time to share exciting info with friends and family. Look at it that way. Now it's your turn to truly sell me. And so, this would happen from time to time with various telemarketers. To be perfectly honest with you, I had no intention of ever purchasing anything from any of these telemarketers. But this is different. These are teachable moments. Most people, if they believe for some reason that you may not buy, even if it isn't totally true, will fail themselves before they even start. Even if the person had every intention of making a purchase. You just killed the sale based on your attitude. So, I never told them in advance that I wasn't actually buying shit from them. So, I let them "hit me with their best shot" and fire away. And at the end of the call, I would get excited right along with them. Of course, at that point I would congratulate them on how well they did and for certain if they did that repeatedly they would make more sales. So, when they asked if I was interested, I would reply with, "No. I am in fact not interested in purchasing anything you have." They would often ask, "Then why did you just make me go through all of that?" "Because I knew you could do it for real if you tried. Think of how many missed sales and all the money you can now make because of what you just learned in a few minutes." I can't even begin to list how many different names I have been called throughout these processes. So, the only thing I do, is smile and say, "You're welcome." Because of what I just did, they actually care. Enough to call me names, but at least they care. They're fired up and ready to make some serious money.

Telemarketing, believe it or not is one of the most difficult forms of marketing ever to hit the scene. It actually pisses a lot of people off to get a phone call from a stranger telling them about some shit that they have absolutely no time to listen to. Trust me, I don't envy either side of this. But I will share a little secret with you. Those people who do telemarketing, have no idea what their true potential really is. If you are closing deals all day long with strangers whom you don't know and have no type of relationship with, then you my friend have an ability that most don't. You have the socializing skills of Paris Hilton, with the brains of Einstein. You my friend are Fortune 500 material. Imagine what you can do with people you actually know and have relationships with? It is a transitional skill, that is ideal for a candidate here at AEY MARKETING. If you're that good over the phone, and can sell things to complete strangers, then there's endless opportunity to do the same thing for us, without selling anything. If you are helping businesses with the same skillset, you would be generating a hundred times more business guaranteed while making a lot more money. Afterall, isn't that why we market? It's the money. It's why I do it. Also, so I can have damn near whatever it is I want.

So, I pass this on to you. Doing well is my goal for you and your business. It's the main reason I wake up every single morning and do what it is that I do, as well as I do it. Can anyone run a business? No. But you can. And you do. You have the power, the drive, and the energy to ensure your company is unlike any other. The AEY MARKETING advantage is basically digital steroids for your business. You'll notice the gains in your customer and client base immediately, and the results will stun you.

"I work hard. I never give up. Every day I give 110%. There are no limits to my capabilities. There is nothing I can't achieve. I conquer and dominate all I do. I have no bar. I have no ceilings. I break through barriers. I am unstoppable."

My name is Ethan Erhardt. I <u>AM</u> AEY, and this…is FUCKING MARKETING!

Printed in Great Britain
by Amazon